A Story of the Psalms

Conversation, Canon, and Congregation

V. Steven Parrish

LITURGICAL PRESS

Collegeville, Minnesota

www.litpress.org

1   2   3   4   5   6   7   8

Library of Congress Cataloging-in-Publication Data

Parrish, V. Steven, 1953–
    A story of the Psalms : conversation, canon, and congregation /
V. Steven Parrish.
      p. cm.
    Includes bibliographical references and index.
    ISBN 0-8146-2906-7 (alk. paper)
    1. Bible. O.T. Psalms—Criticism, interpretation, etc. I. Title.

BS1430.52.P37 2003
223'.206—dc21

2003044614

For my parents,
Virgil and Jo Ann Parrish,
who introduced me to the Psalms and congregations
when I was still a child.

Contents

Preface

his book arose from the invitation to deliver the Perry Lectures at Bethel College in McKenzie, Tennessee, January 1999. In particular, I was asked to relate the Book of Psalms and pastoral ministry in ways that might be useful for the clergy who would attend the lectures. Those three lectures, enriched by the lively exchanges with clergy over those two days, form the core of the pages that follow.

I have tried to set recent developments in reading the Book of Psalms and current studies of, largely, North American congregations together in a constructive way. Specifically, there is a movement in some quarters of Psalm scholarship to study the final shape of the Hebrew Psalter for any theological claims that might be made by means of its arrangement and form. In one way or another, most people who pursue this line of study acknowledge that the losses of king, Temple, land, and the Babylonian Exile were crucial in determining the final shape of the Book of Psalms. Simply put, the Psalter addresses this catastrophic episode in Israel's life. In the chapters that follow I build on these insights, but attempt to push a bit beyond the redaction-critical confines. I propose that the Book of Psalms can be thought of as a deeply textured story that is narrated by multiple, and often competing, voices. This story narrates crucial episodes, or moments, in Israel's life and follows a story line that moves through Israel's emergence, establishment, and collapse, to Israel's reemergence. I believe that this approach takes seriously certain aspects of form-critical investigations from the past decades while nudging the study of the Book of Psalms toward a more synchronic direction.

The conversation that takes place in the Book of Psalms comes to communities of faith as Scripture, or canon. As such, it addresses fundamental issues of identity and direction. "Who are we, and what are we to do?" These are the crucial questions that canon engages.

In the estimation of more than a few students of congregations, today's religious communities are intensely engaged in a quest for identity and direction. Increased mobility, Internet, immigration patterns, and secularization have altered congregational ecologies, or contexts. The familiar religious cultures that nurtured many of us in previous years now seem threatened or even inadequate. It is as if we have been transported to a foreign landscape where the guideposts are inscribed with unfamiliar characters and the words we hear sound unintelligible. In many ways, today's congregations are living out the plot of Israel's story in the Psalms.

It is the goal of this book to listen to Israel's story of emergence, establishment, collapse, and reemergence in the Book of Psalms. It is the hope that as we overhear the multiple and often competing conversations that narrate this incredible story, we might also hear a Word of God to help today's congregations in their struggles for identity and purpose.

Many people have contributed to the making of this book and I gratefully acknowledge them (although I hold no one of them accountable for its content!). Bethel College and the Commission on the Ministry of the Cumberland Presbyterian Church extended me the invitation to deliver the Perry Lectures in 1999. The Board of Trustees of Memphis Theological Seminary granted me a sabbatical leave in 2001 that helped me to develop the initial lectures into a book. My friends John Kilzer and Paul Scheirer read earlier versions of the manuscript and offered many insightful comments. The numerous students who have been in Psalms classes that I have taught, along with the myriad church members who have endured the sermons I have preached on the Psalms over the years, deserve my gratitude. I especially name my teacher, mentor, and friend Walter Harrelson, whose influence and insight continue to inspire me well beyond graduate school. The editorial support and assistance from the Liturgical Press—in particular, Mark Twomey, Linda Maloney, and Colleen Stiller—have been outstanding. And finally, for the abiding presence and support of my wife, Tricia, and our daughters, Leah and Lindsey, I am both honored and grateful.

A Story of the Psalms

his book is about a convergence of stories: a story of the Book of Psalms as it is coming to be understood by many people today; a story of congregations where many of us pastor or are "pastored;" and, inescapably, our own personal stories as we bring our unique identities into the reading of Scripture and the participation in one or another religious community. Fruitful biblical interpretation occurs as these stories intersect, intertwine, and engage each other. So, I begin with a personal story.

A Story from My Past

My father was one of ten children who grew up in a farming community of rural southwest Kentucky. Like many children from that time and region, Dad first learned to till and cultivate the land walking behind a team of mules or horses. By the time he was in his mid-teens my Grandfather scraped up enough money to buy an "A" John Deere tractor and implements. One day not long after that, Dad was disking a field with the tractor when a gust of wind blew his felt hat off and right into the path of the disk. Without thinking, Dad shouted: "Whoa!" It was a command that the mules would have understood but one that the John Deere completely ignored. Before he could find the clutch, Dad had disked his hat into the ground.

There was no more to the story than that, and the first time I heard it as a kid I thought it was funny. I could imagine the whole scene as if I had been there, even though it happened years before I was born. I could see him sitting up there on that big, green tractor shouting at it while his hat was being shredded, and I would have to laugh. Every now and then, as the years passed, I'd ask Dad to tell me the story again without really knowing why. He'd repeat it, the scene would reappear in my mind, and I'd chuckle like I did the first time that I heard it.

We've never had a serious discussion about what the story means, or even if it means anything in particular. But as I think about it now— after exchanging my typewriter for a computer; postage stamps and phone calls for e-mail and voice mail; vinyl records for digital CDs—my interest in the story may not have been solely because of its humor. At the very least, it is a story about life lived at transitional moments with the promise and peril that accompany such times. It is a story about competing modes of life, each with its own claims and expectations. It is a story whose ending has to be renegotiated by engaging those competing claims— sometimes at the "drop of a hat." It is a story about identity, and the pressing necessity of understanding clearly who one is and how one responds to life during moments of upheaval and change. At the risk of stretching too far, it is a story that might even make contact with Israel's story in the Psalms and the stories of many congregations entering the twenty-first century.

A Story of the Psalms

Before the 1970s, scholarly study of the Book of Psalms in the twentieth century largely followed the path blazed by Herman Gunkel's form-critical analysis,[1] or Sigmund Mowinkel's variation that he called the "cult-functional" approach.[2] The form-critical model was adapted and re-

---

[1] E.g., Herman Gunkel, *Die Psalmen.* 4th ed. Gottinger Handkommentar zum Alten Testament. Gottingen: Vadenhoeck und Ruprecht, 1926. A good English summary of Gunkel's method may be found in Gunkel, *The Psalms.* Trans. Thomas M. Horner. Facet Books: Biblical Series, 19 (Philadelphia: Fortress, 1967).

[2] Sigmund Mowinckel, *PsalmenStudien.* 2 vols. Oslo: Skrifter utgitt av Det Norske Videnskaps-Adademi I Olso, 1921–24; reprint (Amsterdam: Verlag P. Schippers, 1961). For English readers see Mowinckel, *The Psalms in Israel's Worship.* Two vols. Trans. D. R. Ap-Thomas (Nashville: Abingdon, 1962).

fined over the years, notably by people like Claus Westermann and Erhard Gerstenberger.[3] Each of these scholars, in his own way, was interested to study the structure, form, and setting from which an *individual psalm* arose and/or in which it functioned. To be sure, the ability to claim that a certain "type" or "form" existed—whether a hymn, lament, thanksgiving, etc.—meant that the form had to be evident in more than a single psalm. It was part of Gunkel's genius that he looked for the "typical" features of the various psalms and not simply their unique or singular features. This led him to see recurring patterns that in turn helped him classify psalms into various types. Still, psalm exegesis normally proceeded by studying single psalms in relative isolation from their larger literary context within the Book of Psalms. Much has been gained by these efforts and form criticism continues to be an important dimension of most any study of the Psalms. In fact, I will claim later that form criticism helps us distinguish the distinct, and frequently competing, voices that narrate Israel's story in the Psalms.

By the 1970s biblical scholarship in general was beginning to ask different questions from biblical texts. Broadly speaking, these questions tended to be more about literary context than about the historical context that gave rise to the various forms of literature in the Bible.[4] One can note this shift of interest in Psalms study as early as in a 1976 essay by Brevard Childs.[5] Here Childs raised questions about the shape of the Book of Psalms, canon, inner biblical exegesis, and interestingly, about the superscriptions over many of the psalms.[6] In precritical readings of the

---

[3] E.g., Claus Westermann, *Praise and Lament in the Psalms*. Trans. Keith R. Crim and Richard N. Soulen (Atlanta: John Knox, 1981). Erhard Gerstenberger, *Psalms: Part I*. The Forms of Old Testament Literature, 14 (Grand Rapids: Eerdmans, 1988).

[4] It is customary to date this shift of focus to James Muilenburg's 1968 Presidential Address to the Society of Biblical Literature, later published as: James Muilenburg, "Form Criticism and Beyond," *JBL* 88 (1969) 1–18. Many would also point to the book by Phyllis Trible (*God and the Rhetoric of Sexuality*. OBT. Philadelphia: Fortress, 1978)—one of Muilenburg's former students—as one of the earlier, sustained efforts in biblical studies to move beyond strictly form-critical concerns.

[5] Brevard Childs, "Reflections on the Modern Study of the Psalms," in *Magnalia Dei: The Mighty Acts of God*, ed. Frank M. Cross and others (Garden City, N.J.: Doubleday, 1976) 377–78. See also Childs' slightly later book, *Introduction to the Old Testament As Scripture* (Philadelphia: Fortress, 1979).

[6] Childs, "Reflections."

Psalms, these superscriptions, or titles, frequently had guided exegesis by placing an individual psalm within the framework of Israel's larger narrative—especially the Books of Samuel. Form-critical study deemed the titles as secondary and late, and typically ignored or downplayed their significance in exegesis.

To Childs' credit, he saw that ignoring the titles would not make them go away; after all, they were a part of the finished psalm, and the psalm was a part of the larger canon as we have it. A few years later, Gerald Wilson followed the lead of Childs in his doctoral dissertation and argued that the Book of Psalms is more than a random arrangement of one hundred and fifty individual poems.[7] In Wilson's view, the present shape of the Book of Psalms addressed Israel's experience of monarchy, the loss of kingship, and offered guidance for exilic and postexilic Israel.[8]

On what basis did Wilson arrive at this conclusion? Among other things, he observed that Royal Psalms (psalms that have the Davidic monarchy especially in view) appear at the "seams" of the five-fold division of the Psalter only in Books One through Three (i.e., Psalms 2, 72, 89). In Psalm 2, which stands with Psalm 1 at the head of the Psalter, God declares emphatically, "I have set my king, upon Zion my holy hill" (v. 6). This is a king that the nations can recognize as YHWH's anointed (literally, *měšîaḥ*, or messiah, v. 2), and also reports a divine oracle saying that he was "begotten" by God (v. 7). However we take these lines, it is clear that YHWH and the Davidic king stand "close" at the beginning of the Psalter.

Book Two ends with Psalm 72 that is introduced by the superscription, "Of Solomon." The suggestion is that the arrangement between

---

[7] Subsequently published as, Gerald Wilson, *The Editing of the Hebrew Psalter*, SBLDS 76 (Chico, Calf.: Scholars Press, 1985).

[8] That the final form of the Psalter represents purposeful shaping is so clear (although the precise *meaning* of the shape is up for debate) that the burden of proof would be on those who might argue otherwise. The most obvious pointer is the five-fold division of the Book of Psalms—Psalms 1–41 (Book One); Psalms 42–72 (Book Two); Psalms 73–89 (Book Three); Psalms 90–106 (Book Four); Psalms 107–150 (Book Five). Clearly the remark at the end of Psalm 72 once marked the conclusion of a group of Davidic psalms: "The Prayers of David son of Jesse are ended." One could mention groupings of psalms that prefer the divine name YHWH (Pss 3–41) and other groupings that prefer the divine name Elohim (Pss 51–72). For a succinct discussion of these and other indicators of the intentional shaping of the Psalter see Klaus Seybold, *Introducing the Psalms*, trans. R. Graeme Dunphy (Edinburgh: T&T Clark, 1990) 1–33.

YHWH and David is passed on to his son and successor, Solomon, after which the prayers of David come to an end (72:20). All still seems to bode well for the Davidic monarchy. Even the ending of Book Three begins well enough. Psalm 89:1-37 remembers God's enduring covenant with David, but only to acknowledge in the next breath that God has rejected David (vv. 38 ff.). The psalm and Book Three end on discordant notes that question God's allegiance to David. What might lead to such intense questioning? At least one likely answer looms large: the collapse of the Davidic monarchy after the destruction of Jerusalem by the Babylonians in 587 B.C.E.

Intriguingly, Book Four opens with a psalm introduced by the superscription: "A prayer of Moses, the man of God" (Ps 90). This is the only superscription in the Book of Psalms that specifically mentions Moses. If there was any star on Israel's horizon larger than David, then surely it was Moses. The beginning of Book Four remembers that there was a time before land, kings, and palaces. It hints that before Mt. Zion there had been another sacred mountain. Before the wilderness of Babylonian Exile, there had been another wilderness through which Israel had been guided without king by pillars of fire, clouds, and the Ark to reunite with an earlier promise made to Abraham. Before kings and temples there was YHWH, and in staccato fashion Book Four reminds a new wilderness generation: the Lord reigns (Pss 93, 95–99). The answer to the dismal ending of Book Three is the affirmation of YHWH's reign that will call for, in Book Five (Pss 107–159), trust in YHWH.[9]

Although this brief summary does not do justice to it, Wilson's publication has generated considerable interest in the canonical shape of the Book of Psalms and captured the attention of many scholars.[10] Although not everyone would agree on all of the details, there seems to be a broad acknowledgment that the final form of the Book of Psalms represents a response by Israel to the losses of king, temple, land, and the ensuing

---

[9] See especially Wilson, *Editing*, 199–228.

[10] For example, James L. Mays, "The Place of the Torah-Psalms in the Psalter," *JBL* 106 (1987) 3–12; Walter Brueggemann, "Bounded by Obedience and Praise: The Psalms as Canon," *JSOT* 50 (1991) 63–92; J. Clinton McCann, Jr., *A Theological Introduction to the Book of Psalms* (Nashville: Abingdon, 1993); J. Clinton McCann, Jr., ed. *The Shape and Shaping of the Psalter*, JSOTSup 159 (Sheffield: Sheffield Academic Press, 1993); Nancy L. de-Claisse-Walford, *Reading from the Beginning: The Shaping of the Hebrew Psalter* (Macon, Ga.: Mercer University Press, 1997).

Babylonian Exile after 587 B.C.E. To put it another way, one can hear in the Psalter voices that remember the emergence of Israel, the establishment of monarchy, the collapse of monarchy, and the reemergence of Israel. In essence, there is a story-like movement in the final form of the Psalter that will be an undergirding assumption for the pages that follow.

It is also noteworthy that the canonical study of the Book of Psalms has been pursued along two basic lines associated with the names of Brevard Childs and James Sanders. A detailed analysis of these two tacks need not be repeated here.[11] It is sufficient to note that Childs believes the final form of the Psalter intentionally obscures the processes that led to its production. Without denying that the individual psalms functioned in specific contexts before they were gathered into small groupings that were in turn gathered into increasingly larger groupings, readers should take their interpretive cue from the final form of the Psalter.[12] In contrast, Sanders is interested in the processes that gave shape to the canon, the shape of the canon at various stages in its growth, and the dialectical relationship between the community that produced the texts and the texts that shaped the community.[13]

It could be argued that Childs's approach avoids the risks of uncertainty associated with any act of historical reconstruction, but it offers a less textured reading than Sanders's model. On the other hand, Sanders's approach has a multidimensional depth to it but runs the dangers presented by reconstructing a historical process that is obscured by the text itself. What both scholars hold in common is their belief that the Psalter possesses the status of canon. Whether in an earlier and different shape, or in its later and final form, the collection(s) of the Psalms represent an authoritative, theological source from which to find guidance for life.

Is there any way to take the best from these two distinct approaches into a study of the Psalms? It strikes me that many of the insights gained from narrative analysis of the Bible over the past few years may offer a somewhat novel and productive way of reading the Book of Psalms.

[11] For a succinct and useful summary of Childs's and Sanders's approaches see de-Claisse-Walford, *Reading from the Beginning,* 8–14.

[12] See Childs, *Introduction to the Old Testament as Scripture.*

[13] See, for example, James A. Sanders, *Canon and Community: A Guide to Canonical Criticism,* Guides to Biblical Scholarship (Philadelphia: Fortress, 1984); *From Sacred Story to Sacred Text* (Philadelphia: Fortress, 1987).

The Psalms, Story, and Narrative

Clearly psalms and narrative are distinct genres and are not to be collapsed into a single literary form. But the two are not mutually exclusive.[14] Perhaps the most obvious example of the compatibility of the two genres is the presence of Psalm 18 as 2 Samuel 22, or the presence of 2 Samuel 22 as Psalm 18, depending upon the direction of influence—a matter not easily settled. However one should decide the issue, a knowledgeable reader of Scripture does not approach 2 Samuel 22 without carrying an awareness of Psalm 18 into the act of reading, and vice versa. The point I make is that narrative accommodates poetry, and poetry accommodates narrative.

But we can shift from the intertextual connections between entire compositions like Psalm 18 and 2 Samuel 22 to the interior workings of biblical poetry itself. To read Psalm 18 is to move from an affirmation of YHWH's rock-solid reliable character (vv. 1-3), to a terrifying confrontation with death (vv. 4-5), to a cry for help to God who listens (v. 6), and who responds by shaking the heavens and earth and drawing the psalmist from the "mighty waters" (vv. 7-19). Clearly the progression is from conflict to resolution. Shimon Bar-Efrat describes plot, a fundamental element of narrative, as "an organized system of events, arranged in temporal sequence. . . . the plot of a narrative is constructed as a meaningful chain of interconnected events."[15] With its movement from conflict to resolution Psalm 18 clearly exhibits a "meaningful chain of interconnected events."[16] Quite simply, it has a plot.

We can move yet closer to the workings of biblical poetry. One of the most visible characteristics of biblical poetry is the way that parts of a poetic verse complement one another—a feature called parallelism. Robert Alter has described the movement that can occur between parts of verses and shown how poetry can exhibit a kind of narrativity.[17] Such movement

[14] On the distinction between poetry and prose, one should not forget James Kugel's counsel. Although he may have overstated the case, the lines between poetry and prose are not always as neat as some would like to draw them. See James L. Kugel, *The Idea of Biblical Poetry* (New Haven: Yale University Press, 1981).

[15] Shimon Bar-Efrat, *Narrative Art in the Bible*, JSOTSup 70 (Sheffield: The Almond Press, 1989) 91.

[16] Ibid.

[17] Robert Alter, *The Art of Biblical Poetry* (New York: Basic Books, 1985), see especially the chapter "From Line to Story" on 27–71. See also Robert Alter, "Psalms," *The Literary*

might be temporal (e.g., from Monday to Tuesday) or sequential (e.g., from sickness to health, or even from sin to sickness as the ancients often thought). For example, Psalm 18:3 reads:

> I call upon the Lord, who is worthy to be praised,
> so I shall be saved from my enemies (NRSV).[18]

In the first half of the verse the psalmist "calls" upon a praiseworthy God. If the verse stopped there, one might wonder the reason for the call or even why God is worthy of praise. But the verse continues. The poet's call reveals a threat from enemies (hence, the reason for the call) and an acknowledgment that God saves those who call out (the reason God is praiseworthy). Within this single verse there is a narrative sequence from calling out, to being saved.[19] As it happens, this sequence mirrors precisely the narrative movement of the entire psalm.

While Alter is clear to state that narrativity is not to be equated with narrative,[20] these remarks show that the gulf between poetry and narrative may not be as vast as sometimes imagined. If this narrative impulse that characterizes poetry is set within the framework of an overarching sequential and temporal movement such as the one described by Wilson, may we not think, then, of the Book of Psalms itself as exhibiting a narrative, story-like character? Without using the specific words "narrative" or "story," Roland Murphy acknowledges that "editorial arrangement can suggest an overall perspective for the Psalter."[21] It will be my assumption in the pages that follow that the "overall perspective" of the Book of Psalms as generally described by Wilson, allowing for some modifications, displays a narrative movement that invites the reading of the Psalter

---

Guide to the Bible, ed. Robert Alter and Frank Kermode (Cambridge, Mass.: The Belknap Press of Harvard University Press, 1987) 244–62.

[18] Unless noted, as here, all quotations from the Bible will be the author's own translations. Sometimes these translations will be rather "wooden" to capture the force of the original syntax and rhetoric.

[19] W. H. Bellinger, Jr. has in fact used the designation "plot" to describe the movement within psalms, and particularly the movement from crisis to resolution. See, Bellinger, *Psalms: Reading and Studying the Book of Praises* (Peabody, Mass.: Hendrickson, 1990) 36.

[20] Alter, *The Art of Biblical Poetry,* 39.

[21] Roland E. Murphy, *The Gift of the Psalms* (Peabody, Mass.: Henrickson, 2000) 19.

as story.[22] It is important to remember that this perspective, or plot, has been discerned by listening to specific voices (i.e., psalms). That is, a plot arises from attending to certain psalms themselves and should not be viewed as materializing from thin air.[23] The challenge in what follows will be to admit more voices into the telling of this story and listen to the textured nuances they add to the whole.

[22] Although I tend to use the terms "story" and "narrative" rather interchangeably, I prefer story for this project. David M. Gunn and Danna Nolan Fewell acknowledge both the close relationship, and the potential distinctions, between the two words when they write: "The terms 'story' and 'narrative' are often used interchangeably, though sometimes 'the story' is a broader term, understood as the events presupposed by 'the narrative' which tells the story in a particular way" (*Narrative in the Hebrew Bible*, The Oxford Bible Series [Oxford: The Oxford University Press, 1993] 2). To attempt an analogy, a story might be thought of as the urgent and spontaneous words a hospital chaplain hears upon visiting a patient just diagnosed with a life-threatening illness. The exchange between chaplain and patient is what is represented in a good verbatim, although a verbatim already lies at least one step removed from the patient's experience itself, and probably reflects at least a minimal amount of selectivity and structuring. A narrative would represent the more stylized and systematic representation of those words by the chaplain who tries to make sense and meaning from the exchange. This formal recasting of the exchange approaches what one might find in a carefully written case study. Both presentations deal with the raw edges of life and death but, given this distinction, story lives a bit closer than narrative. The Book of Psalms lives close to the exposed nerves of human existence. (I am grateful to my colleague in pastoral care, Lee Ramsey, for discussions about the connections between story and pastoral care.)

[23] James L. Crenshaw has recently reviewed efforts to locate meaning in the shape of the Psalter and has described the effort as "largely subjective" (Crenshaw, *The Psalms: An Introduction* [Grand Rapids: Eerdmans, 2001] 98). He is, of course, correct and I agree that canonical studies along with the narrative / story approach that I am proposing make subjective decisions. But the different conclusions reached by historical-critical scholars like Sigmund Mowinckel, Artur Weiser, Claus Westermann, Hans Joachim-Kraus, and Erhard Gersteberger admit no small amount of subjectivity in their own work. It is important to remember that subjectivity is inescapable; it is not necessarily evil; and it can possess methodological rigor. Gerald Wilson has offered guidance in arguing that it is importance to distinguish between the "indicators" of the Psalter's shape and the "significance" of the shape. Significance arises by attending to specific features of the text that, in turn, suggest significance. See, Gerald H. Wilson, "The Shape of the Book of Psalms," *Interpretation* (April 1992) 129–42.

Conversation

Roland Murphy, following the lead of others, has spoken of prayer as "conversation with God."[24] The prayers in the Book of Psalms are surely this, but they are also more. While the individual praises and prayers engage God, they also engage one another so that in the Book of Psalms there are both vertical and horizontal dimensions. There is a conversation between psalmist and psalmist, as well as between psalmist and God, to be overheard in the Psalter.

Importantly, not all of the Psalms have the same thing to say. For example, Psalm 2 affirms God's protection of the Davidic king. But if we allow the superscription of Psalm 3 to guide our reading of it, in the next breath David is on the lam because his own son Absalom is out to kill him. It can be argued that the question posed by Psalm 89 at the end of Book Three, which begins with a bold affirmation of God's covenant with David and concludes with a poignant inquiry about what has become of that covenant, is foreshadowed by the juxtaposition of Psalms 2 and 3. In Psalm 2 God laughs at enemies of the anointed king; in Psalm 3 it appears that the enemies are near to having the last laugh: "A Psalm of David, *when he fled from his son Absalom*" (Ps 3, superscription; emphasis added). The movement from Psalm 2 to Psalm 3 is jarring and filled with tension.

As Israel's story goes, so go the Psalms. Although one can detect an overall plot to the book, the story is told by distinct voices often at odds with one another. Form criticism has taught us, with its distinctions between hymns, laments, thanksgivings, etc., that not all psalms, or voices, are alike. Any story narrated by the individual psalms is far from straightforward, but interesting stories rarely are straightforward. They are filled with twists and turns that tantalize and entice the reader forward. To appreciate the depth and rich texture of the Psalter's story, it is important to invite as many distinct voices as possible to the seminar table, or the church school class room, or the Tuesday evening small group meeting. Walter Brueggemann contends that ". . . to value fully any psalm, it must be used in the context of all of them."[25] Although practical reasons make it virtually inconceivable to imagine all of the possible conversations that

---

[24] Murphy, *The Gift of the Psalms*, 58.

[25] Walter Brueggemann, *The Message of the Psalms: A Theological Commentary*, Augsburg Old Testament Studies (Minneapolis: Augsburg Publishing Company, 1984) 16.

might take place among the 150 psalms in the Hebrew Psalter, Brueggemann's point is important. To sense and appreciate any sort of story in the Book of Psalms, it is urgent to attend to as many voices as possible and especially critical to hear those conversation partners that may be underrepresented and that may run against the grain of the status quo.

Canon

The conversation within the Book of Psalms is no ordinary conversation, and so the story narrated is no ordinary story. The Psalter comes to us as a part of the *canon* of Scripture. To acknowledge this status is to grant an authoritative edge to the Psalter and to recognize in it a special conversation that helps organize our lives in relation to God and to one another. More pointedly, as James Sanders writes, canon ". . . serves to engage the two questions: who am I, or we, and what are we to do? . . . Canon functions, for the most part, to provide indications of the identity as well as the life style of the ongoing community that reads it."[26]

On the one hand, canon is anchored in the past. A cultural artifact—whether oral story, text, or icon—becomes canonical only when it is "reused" by an individual or a community that is struggling for a sense of identity and direction.[27] Frequently it is a crisis that gives rise to such urgent struggles and leads to an inventory of resources that have proved useful in previous times of turmoil. Sanders writes that in such moments

> . . . only the old, tried and true has any real authority. . . . A new story will not do; only a story with old, recognizable elements has the power for life required, because it somehow can pierce beneath the immediate and apparent changes taking place to recover the irreducible core of identity left unthreatened, that which can survive the crisis.[28]

That which is deemed canonical has the power to provide stability and establish order in situations of crisis.[29]

---

[26] James A. Sanders, "Adaptable for Life: The Nature and Function of Canon," in *From Sacred Story to Sacred Text* (Philadelphia: Fortress, 1987) 17.

[27] Sanders, "Adaptable for Life," 16.

[28] Ibid., 21.

[29] It is important to remember that canon can also function to destabilize a community. This can be seen particularly in the rhetoric of the prophets. For example, Amos

On the other hand, canon lunges forward into the future. Because of its past utility canon is able to project, at least within broad contours, the shape a community must take for survival in the future. This process *may* call for a replication of the past. Jeremiah's plea for the people to "return" to God may suggest as much (e.g., Jer 4:1-2). But appeals to authoritative traditions merely to redo the past are uncharacteristic of Israel's theologians.[30] More often than not, canonical memories call for the reshaping of the present community. This is particularly evident in the prophetic message contained in Isaiah 40–55, where the prophet invokes the ancient Exodus memory and calls for the Babylonian exiles to imagine new possibilities and to live accordingly. The people may feel like "withered grass," but they are urged by the prophet to hear some good news (Isa 40:6-11). The new Exodus that awaits them will outstrip the former one (Isa 43:16-21). Such a proclamation, anchored in the past, calls for a reshaping of the exilic community. Walter Brueggemann has clearly noted the power of Israel's story contained in the historical psalms (Pss 78, 105, 106, 126)—a power that can both make and unmake worlds.[31] Canon goes beyond merely identifying a community or assisting it to sing the same old song. Canon can lead to new songs that give new direction and reshape communities. It defines, but it also reshapes. In their discussion of stories, Gunn and Fewell capture this dual focus when they write:

---

draws upon the "canonical" story of the Exodus to remind a complacent Northern Kingdom that God has worked similar feats for other people, and thereby challenges a false sense of security in the Mosaic covenant (Amos 9:7-8). With a similar move, Jeremiah reminds his audience that a thoughtless and static reliance upon the physical presence of the Jerusalem Temple is tragically misguided when he appeals to the living memory of ancient Shiloh's destruction (Jeremiah 7). By way of these efforts, the prophets sought to upset the status quo and urge a new sense of direction.

[30] A good discussion of the dynamic character of Israel's authoritative, or "paradigmatic," traditions may be found in Paul D. Hanson's discussion of community (*The People Called*. San Francisco: Harper & Row, 1986). Hanson argues that moving ancient notions into the present typically calls for certain adaptations. Even authoritative notions possess an inherent dynamism if they are to remain authoritative. This is not unlike the point that Sanders makes in his discussion of canon ("Adaptability").

[31] Walter Brueggemann, *Abiding Astonishment: Psalms, Modernity, and the Making of History*, Literary Currents in Biblical Interpretation (Louisville: Westminster/John Knox, 1991) 21–28.

Stories order and reorder our experience; that is to say they *reveal* the way things are in the real world. They reflect a given culture. Alternatively, stories may be thought to *create* the real world. They are "performative" rather than simply explanatory. They give meaning to life, implicitly making proposals for thought and action which are then embodied in a re-created world.[32]

In the case of the exilic prophet, the recreated world is one of hope and liberation rather than one of despair and bondage, and the challenge is how to live with such a vision.

Of all that one might say about the concept of canon, the notion of identity is fundamental. It is this notion that finds expression in the Book of Psalms. The many individual voices join one another in an ongoing conversation. The conversation is deeply focused upon the experiential moment from which the psalmists speak, but it draws from the past and looks to the future. This conversion between different moments is poignantly captured in the baleful cry of "How long, O Lord?" (Ps 13:1-2). The singer of this desperate song cries out from a moment of pain knowing that life has not always been so anguished and yearning for a time when equilibrium will be restored. Past, present, and future are caught up in the thick merger of moments and are given voice through a question. It is a question that searches for identity, for purpose; it is a question that is sounded many times over in the Psalms; it is a question that joins other questions, as well as affirmations, that tell about Israel's emergence, establishment, collapse, and reemergence.

Congregation

Those who study congregations underscore the importance of a congregation's awareness of its own identity and its understanding of the context in which it is located. These twin pillars of a congregation's existence have recently been called, respectively, "culture" and "ecology."[33] By her use of the word "culture," Nancy Ammerman intends to challenge popular notions of identity as something fixed. She writes that ". . . thinking about a congregation's culture reminds us that it is something that this

---

[32] Gunn and Fewell, *Narrative in the Hebrew Bible*, 1.

[33] See Nancy T. Ammerman and others, eds., *Studying Congregations: A New Handbook* (Nashville: Abingdon, 1998) especially chs. 2 and 3.

group of people has created, not a fixed or normative category. Unlike our usual notions about identity, a culture is neither who we always will be nor who we ought to be."[34] She does not mean that congregational culture is created *ex nihilo*. Congregations are always a part of a larger tradition that they receive and, in turn, convey. But they interact with the inherited tradition in a lively way so that a congregation is ". . . always a mix of local creativity and larger tradition."[35] To speak of the context in which a congregation is located as "ecology" is to see the congregation "as a unit interacting with other units in society: people, organizations, and cultures."[36] Understood in these ways, culture (identity) and ecology (context) are characterized by a high degree of dynamism.

Few people would deny that congregations find themselves in contexts that have changed, and are changing, with blinding speed. Formerly large metropolitan churches, once surrounded by members within walking distance, find themselves with pews to spare and deserted by their founding ancestors who have moved to the suburbs. Other congregations that once were situated in quiet, rural valleys increasingly find themselves swallowed by creeping urban sprawl. Churches once viewed as the moral guardians of their communities find themselves engulfed in scandals arising from immoral actions by their religious leaders.

Additionally, the world truly has become a smaller place. For example, Nancy L. Eiesland and R. Stephen Warner observe that

> Crackdowns on dissidents in Cuba result in increased immigration to Miami; economic downturns in Mexico spur increased immigration along the border; and opportunities for American college graduates to teach English as a second language in the Czech Republic create an expatriate glut in Prague. Air travel, Internet connections, and educational exchanges have altered the contexts within which we live.[37]

It is no stretch to say that many congregations are struggling for their bearings in a disorienting storm of change.

[34] Nancy T. Ammerman, "Culture and Identity in the Congregation," in *Studying Congregations*, 78.

[35] Ibid., 79.

[36] Nancy L. Eiesland and R. Stephen Warner, "Ecology: Seeing the Congregation in Context," in Ammerman, *Studying Congregations*, 40.

[37] Eiesland and Warner, "Ecology," 42.

In an immensely suggestive study, Loren B. Mead has described the disorientation of today's congregations by sketching broadly three periods of the Church's life. Mead first identifies an "Apostolic Paradigm" that characterizes the Church in the early generations after Jesus. During this relatively brief era of the Church, the boundary between the Church and the world was at the individual congregation's very doors. The mission activity of the Church was carried out in a world generally hostile to the Gospel.[38]

This situation changed, however, with the conversion of Constantine in 313 C.E. At this juncture in time, Christianity became the official religion of the state. The tacit, if not explicit, assumption was that everyone within the State was also within the Church. The mission frontier no longer lay at the doors of the congregation but rather at the boundary of the Empire. Congregations no longer existed within a hostile environment, but a hospitable one. This Mead calls the "Christendom Paradigm." Of course, responding to mission called for different organizational patterns and relationships between local congregations and the larger Church.[39]

In a very important observation Mead notes that one of the weaknesses of the Christendom Paradigm ". . . was its assumption that there was *one* answer, *one* way."[40] Surely the history of the Church, with its multiple councils and creeds, indicates that competing voices always existed and demanded the attention of the Church's leadership. In fact, the same can be said of the earlier Apostolic period. Paul's argument for a particular model of Christianity as opposed to alternative models acknowledges the diversity that characterized the early Church. Likewise, each of the Gospels seems to have in view a specific Christian community with its own unique contours and needs. Fundamental issues about the identity of the Church in its local manifestations were never as firmly and completely settled as the religious leadership hoped and sometimes believed.

In Mead's view, the Christendom Paradigm has now collapsed. He has no name for the emerging paradigm, but it is characterized by the recognition that we can no longer assume that members of the Church and the State are one and the same. The local congregation no longer exists in a world where everyone on the block is hospitable to the Gospel

---

[38] Loren B. Mead, *The Once and Future Church: Reinventing the Congregation for A New Mission Frontier* (Washington, D.C.: The Alban Institute, 1991) 9–13.

[39] Mead, *Once and Future,* 13–17.

[40] Ibid., 17.

message. Mission is no longer limited to the border of a foreign frontier but is found at the very doors of each congregation, and is increasingly a concern of the laity as much as the ordained clergy. In fact, in many ways the situation of the modern Church has remarkable similarities to the Apostolic Paradigm.[41]

Mead's insights are helpful because they offer us a broad pattern that gives a sense of movement. But they are simultaneously disconcerting because they leave us with no small amount of uncertainty about direction. The disorientation experienced by congregations suddenly caught up in their rapidly evolving ecologies has been compared by some to Israel's experience in Babylonian Exile.[42] With all of the landmarks changed, how does a group of people discern its own identity and then respond to a new and chaotic set of circumstances? It is the dilemma posed by the Psalmist's query, "How are we to sing the song of YHWH upon ground that is foreign?" (Ps 137:4). I would suggest that it is precisely here that the story of today's congregations converges with Israel's story in the Book of Psalms.

A Convergence of Stories

Israel's story that is narrated in the Book of Psalms and Mead's brief story of the shifting paradigms in the Church exhibit some intriguing parallels. The convergence of these two stories might be conveniently sketched like this:

Table One: A Story of the Psalms

COLUMN A	COLUMN B	COLUMN C	COLUMN D
Introductory Psalms 1, 2	Books 1–2	Book 3	Books 4–5
Emergence— Mosaic Faith	Establishment— Davidic Monarchy	Collapse— Babylonian Exile	Reemergence— YHWH Reigns
Struggle for Existence	Bold Confidence	Intense Questions and Disorientation	Affirmation in the Midst of Exile

[41] Mead, *Once and Future,* 17–27.

[42] Loren B. Mead, *Five Challenges for the Once and Future Church* (Washington, D.C.: The Alban Institute, 1996), 81–86. See also the volume by Charles H. Bayer, *The Babylonian Captivity of the Mainline Church* (St. Louis: Chalice Press, 1996).

Table Two: A Story of the Church

COLUMN A	COLUMN B	COLUMN C	COLUMN D
Emergence— Apostolic Paradigm	Establishment— Christendom Paradigm	Collapse—Demise of Christendom	Reemergence— ??
Struggle for Existence	Bold Confidence	Intense Questions and Disorientation	??

Note the correspondences between the two tables. *Column A* highlights moments of emergence. Although the Book of Psalms seems to begin with monarchy full-blown and flourishing, Psalm 1, with its stress upon Torah fidelity, surely hints of an earlier time. The emphasis upon two ways (the ways of the wicked and the righteous—verses 6-7) and the urging to choose one way make Psalm 1 strikingly reminiscent of the Book of Deuteronomy. Significantly, Deuteronomy stands at a transitional moment in time and place in the canon; it remembers the past but also looks to the future and represents an important moment in the movement from Mt. Sinai to Mt. Zion. In a similar manner, Psalm 1 introduces Israel's story in the Psalms—a story deeply concerned with kingship; but in doing so it glances backwards to an earlier time of its emergence. Its admission that there are two ways with deeply competing claims suggests that those who choose the way of YHWH will face opposition.[43] This moment in Israel's existence is not unlike the moment in the Church's existence described by Mead as the Apostolic Paradigm.

Column B underscores moments of establishment. David reigns in Jerusalem; Constantine is the Emperor. With David and his successors, the boundaries between the Palace and Temple increasingly diminish. With Constantine and his successors, the boundaries between Church and State indistinguishably blur. These are times of bold confidence, at least for those in the upper echelons of the political and religious establishments.

Column C concerns moments of collapse. The end of Book Three of the Psalter questions the demise of the Davidic monarchy (Ps 89). The destruction of Jerusalem and the Temple, the deportations of 597 and

---

[43] This is not unlike J. Clinton McCann's claim in his discussion of Psalms 1 and 2. Although ". . . God's reign is proclaimed as a present reality . . . it is always experienced by the faithful amid opposition" (McCann, "The Book of Psalms," *NIB* [Nashville: Abingdon, 1996] 665).

587 B.C.E., were catastrophic beyond description. Even though Israel's (and later, Judah's) size and military potential were not great by most standards, the imperialist expansions of Assyria in the eighth century and of Babylonia in the sixth century (followed by the subsequent Persian, Greek, and Roman Empires)—given Israel's geographical location between the Asian and African continents—increasingly brought the small nation into the international spotlight. The world had "grown smaller" for Israel, and old ways of life collapsed under the weight of new and gargantuan pressures. The collapse of state and faith in Israel occasioned by the Exile, is not unlike the demise of Christendom described by Mead. Intense disorientation and questioning characterize this period and lead to the next.

Column D is concerned with reemergence. As suggested earlier, Israel's story in the Psalter envisions a return to the Mosaic faith where YHWH, not David, reigns. In this affirmation lies the resilience of Israel's faith and existence. No specific program or template is offered by which to reconstruct Israel's social organization. But the intense cry of "YHWH reigns!" is a call for Israel to reexamine its core identity. Who is Israel, and what is Israel to do in a radically changed environment? It is a "canonical question" that returns to a "canonical answer." It is a return to an old story that must be renegotiated in different circumstances: The Lord reigns. This is the stuff of canon.[44]

In Mead's schema, the Church has not adequately responded to the chaos and disorientation resulting from the ecology in which it finds itself.[45] Column D of Table Two remains largely a question mark. We are living in a time when there are glimpses and glimmers of an emerging Church, but also a great amount of uncertainty and searching. Is there a Word of the Lord to be overheard by listening to Israel's story in the Psalms? As our stories engage Israel's story, are there words of guidance that help our congregations creatively and constructively engage their

[44] Sanders, "Adaptable for Life," 21.

[45] More recently, Mead has identified in some detail the chaos of today's congregations: membership and financial losses; a social environment in which denominational loyalties, religious institutions and programs are not considered important by people who deem themselves religious; potential tax policies concerning deductions and property taxes; medical and legal costs; clergy education costs; etc. (Loren Mead, *Transforming Congregations for the Future* [Washington, D.C.: The Alban Institute, 1994] 1–23).

current contexts? A guiding assumption in what follows is that as we listen to the story of the Book of Psalms, we may well overhear a word that helps us discern more sharply the Church that God is calling us to be.

A Palace with Windows: Competing Voices

Among the Ras Shamra (ancient Ugarit) tablets discovered in the 1920s comes a cycle of stories about the Canaanite deity Baʿal. The first part of the cycle contains the exploits of Baʿal and his battle against the chaotic forces of Yam and Nahar (Sea and River). Aided by magical incantations and special weapons provided by Baʿal's artisans, Baʿal defeats Yam and Nahar and dispels chaos from his realm. The next part describes the construction of Baʿal's palace. With some persuasion the high god El grants the right for Baʿal to have a palace built in recognition of the victorious deity's entitlement to power. During the construction project, Baʿal's architects ask if he wants windows in his place, to which he gives a resounding "No!" Apparently Baʿal's initial reasoning is that darkness and boredom are preferable to the threat of enemies sneaking in through open windows when his back is turned. An impermeable world, for all of its drawbacks, is at least a safe world. However, after some thought upon the matter, Baʿal changes his mind, windows are installed, and before too much time passes he again finds himself locked in a mortal struggle (in part three of the cycle) with Mot, death. So it goes with kings, palaces, walls, and windows.[46] Any engagement with voices outside the palace walls runs the risk of challenge and conflict. Despite the considerable force of royal rhetoric and power, there are always dissenting voices that wear away the false veneer of pretentious claims.

I recall this ancient story to return to Mead's elegant claim that the Christendom Paradigm was never as monolithic and unified as religious leaders might wish to have believed.[47] There were always dissenting voices that the hierarchy had to contend with in one way or another. This recognition will be quite relevant for the story we hear in the Psalms. Regardless of the moment of the story that is discussed—whether emergence,

---

[46] For this story, see John C. L. Gibson, ed., *Canaanite Myths and Legends* (Edingurgh: T&T Clark, 1977); Michael David Coogan, *Stories from Ancient Canaan* (Philadelphia: Westminster, 1978).

[47] Mead, *Once and Future,* 17.

establishment, collapse, or reemergence—there will be voices that "do not fit" and argue in a different direction. As seen earlier, Psalm 2 may evoke notions of establishment with its note about Yhwh's king on Zion (v. 6), but the superscription of Psalm 3 offers the disconcerting glimpse of David on the run from his son Absalom, who wants to "disestablish" his father. Like the Canaanite god Baʿal discovered in the old mythic texts, all of the royal rhetoric and recognition that kings might muster does not eliminate alternative (and often frightening!) possibilities.

This story that we will hear in the Book of Psalms is not one that is narrated in a sealed vault. It is a story told in a room with many windows through which the light and the voices from the outside world flow in and are allowed to mingle. The architects of the canonical shape of the Book of Psalms have provided many windows and voices.

It is also important to note that various congregations who listen to the story emerging from the Psalter may locate themselves at one or another moment in Israel's story. Mead's sketch of the Church's movement tends to locate all congregations in a present and uncertain moment. Right or wrong, any number of congregations located in today's ecology may have a very clear sense of identity and direction. That is, the portrait of one congregation may reveal the wrinkles of disarray and collapse, while the biography of another congregation on the next street corner or at the next crossroads may offer exuberant talk about emergence and future possibilities.

Procedure

The following chapters will examine major moments of Israel's story as told by the Book of Psalms. In turn, the periods of emergence, establishment, collapse, and reemergence will be studied. Within each period, multiple voices (i.e., different psalms) that stand in ideological tension and that make competing claims will be called upon to tell their part of the larger story. The goal of this audition is not necessarily to dissolve the tension between rival claims by opting for one voice while silencing the other. After all, the final editors of the Psalter make no such move. Creative theological reflection and creative options for life are best negotiated dialectically. Decisions arrived at are always temporary and must be revisited, renegotiated again and again.

It will be obvious to many readers that I am much influenced by the work of Walter Brueggemann. His use of the categories *orientation, disorientation,* and *new orientation* quickly come to mind and are similar to my designations of *establishment, collapse,* and *reemergence.*[48] There are substantial differences, however. Brueggemann's use of the categories in his *The Message of the Psalms* is guided especially by the form critical work of Claus Westermann and his distinctions between descriptive praise, declarative praise, and lament.[49] For Brueggemann, descriptive praise contributed to the stable orientation of a world, lament expressed the disorientation of a world in disarray, and declarative praise gave specific thanksgiving for divine actions that provided a new possibility and new orientation. Because the 150 psalms are not canonically ordered by this particular schema he must hop about the Psalter quite a bit. Thus, Brueggemann opens his examination of psalms of orientation by moving from Psalm 145, to Psalm 104, to Psalm 33, to Psalm 8, etc. What I am proposing honors the canonical arrangement of the Psalms and allows for a diversity of expression at any given moment in the Psalter's story, which is a very different program.

More than specific categories or terms (as suggestive as they typically are), it is Brueggemann's dialectical approach that runs through so much of his work that I find helpful.[50] Few committee meetings that I have attended have made decisions about important matters through consensus. Further, I suspect that those decisions that were made by consensus silenced opposing voices through one form of intimidation or another. A dialectical or, if one prefers, dialogical approach that attends to multiple voices and claims seems best suited for a study of the Psalms.

Listening is vital for congregations. A key concern of each chapter will be to overhear Israel's conversation through the monitors of congregational

---

[48] Brueggemann, *The Message of the Psalms.* The categories of disorientation and reorientation have been appropriated by Brueggemann from Paul Ricoeur, as he acknowledges in Walter Brueggemann, "Psalms and the Life of Faith: A Suggested Typology of Function," in *The Psalms and the Life of Faith,* ed. Patrick D. Miller (Minneapolis: Fortress, 1995) 3–32.

[49] See Claus Westermann, *Praise and Lament in the Psalms,* trans. Keith R. Crim and Richard N. Soulen (Atlanta: John Knox, 1981).

[50] See my survey of Brueggemann in Donald K. McKim, ed., *Historical Handbook of Major Biblical Interpreters* (Downers Grove, Ill.: InterVarsity, 1998).

identity and context. Or to turn the proposition around, an aim of each chapter will be to enable congregations to understand their own identities and contexts better by listening to Israel discuss its identity and context. As Robert Schreiter writes, "If the congregation can only connect itself to stories of itself, then a narcissistic loop begins to form that will not give that congregation, in the long run, either a satisfying identity or an ability to negotiate change within its environment."[51] As each unique congregation engages Israel's story, it opens itself to potentially new and creative possibilities. For example, when a congregation in a new Church development situation listens to the competing voices in the Psalms that recount Israel's story of emergence, that congregation may become aware of blind spots previously missed in its youthful enthusiasm. What are the potential dangers that may wait as a new congregation grows, as power becomes increasingly centralized, and as those affected by decisions are pushed farther and farther away from the decision-making processes? These are issues that Israel struggled with socially and theologically—struggles given voice in the Psalms. A congregation engaging that story opens itself to an imaginative moment of insight and possibility. This engagement is an invitation to encounter the living Word of God with all of the wonders and the risks that such encounters bring.

No efforts will be made to describe a "program" that any and every congregation can embrace, for no such program exists. Congregational program arises from the unique identity of each congregation. What will be offered, though, is an invitation for each congregation to listen to Israel's amazing and complex story told in the Psalms and to hold open the possibility that this listening might lead to astonishing and enriching encounters with the God of both Israel and the congregation.

---

[51] Robert J. Schreiter, "Theology in the Congregation: Discovering and Doing," in *Studying Congregations: A New Handbook,* ed., Nancy T. Ammerman, et al. (Nashville: Abingdon, 1998) 28.

2

Emergence

ogether, Psalms 1 and 2 introduce Israel's story in the Book of Psalms. Linkages between the two are well known. Neither psalm has its own superscription, but the two are framed by the word ʾašĕrê ("blessed," or "happy"—1:1; 2:11).[1] This envelope structure surrounds the two psalms within a circle of unity. In addition, there are other lexical connections. In Psalm 1:6 the wicked perish *(tʾbd)*, while in Psalm 2:12 kings who do not subordinate themselves to YHWH and Israel's anointed king also perish *(tʾbd)*. The righteous meditate *(hgh)* on Torah in Psalm 1:2, but the people plot *(hgh)* against YHWH and the king in Psalm 2:1-2.[2] Taken together, the Psalter opens with an alliance—or at the very least, an association—between Torah (Ps 1) and king (Ps 2). It would seem, then, that Israel's story in the Book of Psalms begins with kingship healthy and in full blossom. But the alliance between king and Torah was always a shaky one for Israel. Within each psalm itself, then by the two psalms taken together, and finally by their relationship to other texts, the tenuous relationship between Torah and king may be seen.

---

[1] Because the Hebrew Bible includes the superscriptions in the verse numbering and the English translations do not, there is frequently a discrepancy between the Hebrew and English citations. Unless otherwise indicated, I will use the English verse numbers.

[2] For these and other associations between Psalms 1 and 2, see J. Clinton McCann, Jr., "The Book of Psalms," *NIB*, vol. IV (Nashville: Abingdon, 1996) 664–65, 689.

Walter Brueggemann has described Psalm 1 as a psalm that ". . . reflects the unambiguous structure of life. . . . There is no middle ground, no neutral ground. Life—like the psalm—is organized in a sharp either/or."[3] More recently he has written, "no ambiguity or slippage exists."[4] This is a particularly apt description of the psalm if it is heard as a 'solo act' that intones the fate of the righteous and the wicked. The righteous are like green trees with a rich source of nourishment, while the wicked are like dried up husks that the wind carries where it will. Everything is said and done; indeed, there *is* no middle ground. But if heard as an introduction to the Psalter, one quickly discovers that "there's a whole lot of slipping going on."[5] Slippage can be seen both within the psalm and in its relation to other psalms. In fact, the same observation holds for the bold claims made by Psalm 2.

Internal Ambiguities of Psalms 1 and 2

The focus of Psalm 1 is YHWH's Torah. The noun occurs twice in verse 2 and stands in contrast to the "counsel," the "way," and the "abode" of the wicked described in verse 1. While this would seem to stake out the subject of the psalm quite clearly, the noun is evocative and has a range of possible meanings. For example, the noun Torah seems to relate uniquely to the Decalogue in Exodus 24:12. In Leviticus 6:9, Torah consists of instructions given about presenting the burnt offering. Leviticus 12:7 offers Torah to women in connection with childbirth, and Leviticus 13:59 offers Torah about dealing with leprosy. Deuteronomy 1:5 and 17:18 seem especially to have in mind the material in Deuteronomy when speaking of Torah. Of course, in Israel's memory, Torah is preeminently identified with the first five books of Scripture. This would suggest that while the typical translation of the noun Torah as "law," is not incorrect, it is far too restrictive. The material in Genesis through Deuteronomy certainly contains a myriad of laws about multiple topics, but it also contains a large amount of narrative. This admixture of law and story in the Pentateuch

---

[3] Walter Brueggemann, *The Message of the Psalms: A Theological Commentary* (Minneapolis: Augsburg, 1984) 39.

[4] See Walter Brueggemann, "Bounded by Obedience and Praise," in Patrick D. Miller, ed., *The Psalms and the Life of Faith* (Minneapolis: Fortress, 1995) 191.

[5] To paraphrase Jerry Lee Lewis, "Whole Lotta Shakin' Goin' On," Sun Records, 1956.

gives a wide range of possible meanings for the word Torah that goes far beyond modern legalistic notions of law.[6] Perhaps the best rendering of the word is "instruction."[7]

Clearly, then, a reader entertains a special problem upon opening the Book of Psalms. Simply put, the question "Which Torah?" would be pressing enough if the only options available referred to an identifiable entity from the past (e.g., the Decalogue; instructions concerning sacrifice, childbirth, or leprosy; Deuteronomy, or the Pentateuch). But from a canonical point of view, Psalm 1 opens the Psalter and asks readers to consider subsequent psalms as Torah. The psalm points in two different directions—the past and the future. For the inquisitive reader, the irony is this: Torah is supposed to offer instruction. However, in the case of Psalm 1 it raises questions! If Torah is as important as the rhetoric of the psalm claims, then would the real Torah please stand up?

In commenting upon the functions of ambiguity, Meir Sternberg writes that

> . . . the most basic consist in the manipulation of narrative interest: curiosity, suspense, surprise. The withholding of information about the past, especially if it deforms the plot line—the effect appearing before or without the cause—at once stimulates the reader's *curiosity* about the action, the agents, their life and relations below the surface, the world they inhabit. To make sense of them, he [sic. i.e., the reader] will try to resolve the gaps; failing that, he will look forward to new disclosures, so that a gradual release of clues will keep him happily busy on the horns of ambiguity.[8]

The reader of Psalm 1 then looks first to the past to establish which Torah the psalmist has in mind. But the ambiguity also leads the reader to await future possibilities as to the identity of Torah.

Just as Psalm 1 raises the question, "Which Torah?", Psalm 2 evokes the query, "Which king?" The ambiguity is richly presented in verse 2 as unnamed kings, perhaps to be understood as vassal kings,[9] contemplate

---

[6] On the combination of law and narrative, see Terrence Fretheim, *Exodus*, Interpretation (Louisville: Westminster/John Knox, 1991).

[7] For example, see McCann, "The Book of Psalms," 684.

[8] Meir Sternberg, *The Poetics of Biblical Narrative: Ideological Literature and the Drama of Reading* (Bloomington: Indiana University Press, 1985) 259.

[9] See the brief comment by Roland Murphy, *The Gift of the Psalms* (Peabody, Mass.: Hendrickson, 2000) 72.

rebellion literally "against Y𝐇𝐖𝐇 and against his anointed." To rebel against one is to rebel against the other. So, does the psalm's focus lie upon Y𝐇𝐖𝐇 or the Davidic monarch? Scholarship has pointed to both. Without denying that Psalm 2 makes important claims about Y𝐇𝐖𝐇's sovereignty, Gerald Wilson places more stress upon the royal and Davidic dimensions.[10] Indeed, McCann notes that most scholars in the twentieth century tended to emphasize the Davidic theology in the psalm.[11] However, McCann himself sees the accent to be on the reign of God.[12]

This literary ambiguity mirrors, in some respects, the dilemma that Israel faced during the centuries of monarchy. One might claim that Y𝐇𝐖𝐇 reigns, but the earthly monarch was visibly and physically present. While the average citizen might have acknowledged ultimate accountability to Y𝐇𝐖𝐇, that one's life and livelihood were more immediately determined by the Davidic king. It was a situation ripe for exploitation by avaricious tyrants who sought to promote their own agendas by blurring the lines of distinction between the heavenly and earthly monarch.[13] Life under dual kings made for difficult decisions.

External Ambiguities of Psalms 1 and 2 in Relation to Other Psalms

When heard in relation to other psalms, the bold claim of Psalm 1:1 *ʾašěrê haʾish*—"Happy is the one . . ."—is hard to hold. The five laments that follow the introductory Psalms 1 and 2, punctuated with their cries of "Y𝐇𝐖𝐇, how many are my foes!" (Ps 3:1); "When I call, answer me . . . !" (Ps 4:1); "My words—Give ear, Y𝐇𝐖𝐇 . . . !" (Ps 5:1); et al., clearly indicate that Torah piety is not a magical talisman that wards off calamity. McCann is surely correct when he says that, in the view of Psalm 1, "The prosperity of the righteous is real but hidden. It is an openness to and connectedness with God that sustains life amid all threats."[14] But that is a position that can

---

[10] Gerald Wilson, *The Editing of the Hebrew Psalter*, SBLDS (Chico, Calif.: Scholars Press, 1985) 209–10, 213.

[11] McCann, "The Book of Psalms," 689.

[12] Ibid.

[13] Walter Brueggemann has offered a stimulating discussion of the way that kings were always tempted to exploit religion to legitimate their actions in *Israel's Praise: Doxology against Idolatry and Ideology* (Philadelphia: Fortress, 1988).

[14] McCann, "The Book of Psalms," 687.

be difficult to affirm when caught up in more than a few situations. One only has to think of the Book of Jeremiah. Similar to the Psalter, it opens with an assurance of God's protection in the face of harm. But disbelief and taunting from his hearers, beatings, and death threats eventually lead the prophet to lament "Cursed be the day on which I was born!" (Jer 20:14). Just as the call of Jeremiah cannot be understood fully apart from his laments, and vice versa, Psalm 1 and the ensuing laments must be heard together. The world depicted by Psalm 1, then, is not as settled as it might first appear.

Beyond the internal ambiguities of Psalm 2, its relation to other psalms erodes its bold claims. The juxtaposition of Psalms 2 and 3 is stunning. The divine offer of 2:8 ("Ask from me, and I will give nations as your inheritance") gives way to the superscription of Psalm 3: "A song of David, while fleeing from Absalom his son." Perhaps David would have weighed in on the side of the adage that sometimes it's easier to deal with someone else's children than to deal with your own!

So far this discussion has shown that ambiguities exist within Psalm 1 and Psalm 2, and that there are further ambiguities that arise when the claims of each Psalm are heard in relation to the competing claims of other psalms. We can now return to where this chapter began and take up briefly the shaky relationship between Psalm 1 and Psalm 2.

Israel's story in the Book of Psalms opens with the uneasy union of Torah (Ps 1) and monarchy (Ps 2). Together they mirror two powerful covenant traditions that gave shape to, and were shaped by, Israel. The former is preeminently associated with Moses and Mt. Sinai (see especially Exod 19 ff.); the latter is forever linked to David and Mt. Zion (see 2 Sam 7). The two traditions were typically in conflict in Israel. For example, Micah seems to have been shaped by the Moses/Torah tradition when he proclaimed in the eigth century B.C.E. that "Zion, like a field, will be plowed" (3:12). One would gather that the Davidic/Zion tradition was not terribly formative for Micah! Then of course, the classic illustration of the tension between the two covenant traditions is to be found in Jeremiah 7. A century and a half after Micah, Jeremiah would vigorously announce that the people who trusted solely in the sanctity of the "Temple of YHWH" were grievously mistaken. In the prophet's view, YHWH could get along quite nicely without a temple and Jeremiah pointed to a historical precedent to drive home the point: the destruction of Shiloh years before David ever marched across the landscape of Israel's story (Jer 7:1-15).

How does one account for this ambiguous beginning of Israel's story in the Book of Psalms? To return to Sternberg's observation, we have something of an effect without a clear cause. That is, we have a linkage between Torah and kingship with no history of how such a union came to be. In other words, we have a gap. So as readers we pause to look backward for a cause and a way to close the gap. At the same time we hold the possibility open that some clues will also be found as the reading of the Psalms progresses.[15] Inevitably, the opening of the Book of Psalms directs us to reconsider voices that narrate tales of Israel's emergence.

Intertextuality

This reconsideration will be guided largely by insights from a way of reading texts that is called "intertextuality." It is not my goal to offer here a lengthy or theoretical discussion about the nature of intertextuality. Fine discussions already exist.[16] However, a few comments about this interpretive enterprise are useful, if for no other reason than to offer some justification for associating the texts that are discussed below.

In his 1979 discussion of repetition and theme-words, Michael Fishbane wrote that readers may ". . . be guided or provoked towards certain interpretations on the basis of theme-words recurrent in one or several texts which are thereby brought into association. . . . Through such stylistic means, latent networks of intra-and intertextual meaning may be perceived by an interpreter."[17] As two texts interact with each other, the meaning of each text is nuanced differently than would be the case if either was read alone. Precisely *how* different texts are "brought into association" and then how a *description* of that association is to be guided constitutes the basic fronts on which the theoretical discussions of intertextuality occur.

---

[15] Sternberg, *Poetics,* 259. On notions of cause and effect in narrative, see also Mark Allan Powell, *What Is Narrative Criticism?* Guides to Biblical Scholarship (Minneapolis: Fortress, 1991) 40–42.

[16] See, for example, Richard B. Hays, *Echoes of Scripture in the Letters of Paul* (New Haven/London: Yale University Press, 1989) especially 1–34. A more recent and, for this book, significant study is Beth LaNeel Tanner, *The Book of Psalms Through the Lens of Intertextuality,* Studies in Biblical Literature, 26. (New York: Peter Lang, 2001) especially 5–75.

[17] Michael Fishbane, *Text and Texture: Close Readings of Selected Biblical Texts* (New York: Schocken Books, 1979) xii.

Drawing on the work of several literary theorists, Beth LaNeel Tanner has offered four steps to guide intertextual analysis. First comes the reader's recognition of a "marker" that ". . . may be a direct quotation, a word, a series of words . . . a name, a distorted quotation, a plot element in the story or another indication of an intertextual connection."[18] Second, the reader must be able to identify the "the evoked text . . . Step three involves the interaction of the two texts to form an intertextual pattern . . . Step four . . . involves 'the activation of the evoked text as a whole in an attempt to form maximum intertextual patterns.'"[19] I will not attempt to follow these four steps mechanically, but they will influence the following discussion at a number of points.

Finally, it is important to note the difficulty of intertextual analysis in explaining exactly what evokes a reader's association between texts. Tanner writes that this is "where the individuality and ideology of the reader comes to the forefront."[20] Sometimes an author or editor intentionally draws texts into associations that a reader can sense. This seems almost certainly the case with Job 7:17-18 and Psalm 8:4. But even Richard Hays, whose approach is more "author-centered" than that of many literary critics, writes "that texts can generate readings that transcend both the conscious intention of the author and all the hermeneutical strictures that we promulgate."[21] Perhaps this is the place, then, to acknowledge that exegesis is an imaginative art. It is not haphazard, for there are guidelines, but it is art nonetheless—which is to say that not everyone will likely agree with the rendering that follows.

Which Torah and Which King?
Conversations Among Psalms One, Two, and Deuteronomy 17:14-20

In quest for some answer, the ambiguity in Psalms 1 and 2 about which Torah and which king leads the curious reader to reconsider other texts where Torah and king are brought together. One obvious candidate

---

[18] Tanner, *The Book of Psalms*, 72.

[19] Tanner, 72, 73. For a different set of guidelines, see the seven steps proposed by Richard Hays, *Echoes of Scripture*, 29–33.

[20] Tanner, *The Book of Psalms*, 74.

[21] Hays, *Echoes of Scripture*, 33.

is Deuteronomy 17:14-20—a text that links Torah fidelity and kingship in a remarkable way.

The Book of Deuteronomy is immensely complicated in terms of its origin, redaction, and canonical location. Does the book come from the north? If so, does it derive from Levitical, prophetic, or wisdom circles? How and when did the traditions make their way to the south? Were the traditions compiled shortly before, or during, the Babylonian exile? Or were there at least two periods of intensive editorial activity? Does Deuteronomy belong with the four books that precede it in the canon, or is it more properly related to the books that follow? All of these questions have been intensely debated and are rehearsed in most critical commentaries. The question most relevant for this discussion is the last one: To which group of books does Deuteronomy most closely relate—the preceding ones or the following ones?

Patrick D. Miller describes Deuteronomy as a "boundary" book. On the one hand it concludes what has preceded it, and on the other it introduces the future. In the book, Israel stands between the promises of the past, the Exodus, the wilderness, and the promise of the future: the land. It looks two ways.[22] Miller identifies three audiences to which Deuteronomy may speak: 1) the people who stand waiting to possess the promised gift of land; 2) the people who have lived with the gift and have come to know the struggles of life with the land; 3) the people who have seen the loss of the land to foreign invaders.[23] For this discussion I am most interested in the boundary nature of the book, especially as it pertains to the first audience that Miller identifies—the people who await the land at its very boundary. My decision merely takes the *literary* setting within the book seriously.

With this in mind we turn to Deuteronomy 17:14-20. The association of Psalms 1 and 2 with this text is not a new one. For example, William H. Brownlee has argued that Psalms 1 and 2 together were possibly used at the coronation of a late Judean king to proclaim that "a king who fulfilled the ideal of Psalm 1 would be a good Deuteronomic king."[24]

---

[22] Patrick D. Miller, *Deuteronomy*, Interpretation (Louisville: Westminster/John Knox, 1990) 9–10.

[23] Miller, *Deuteronomy*, 4.

[24] William H. Brownlee, "Psalms 1–2 as a Coronation Liturgy," *Biblica* 52 (1971) 332.

One need not follow Brownlee's cultic/political argument in order to see connections between the two psalms and Deuteronomy 17:14-20.

For one thing, Psalms 1 and 2, when read together, have as their subjects Torah fidelity and kingship. That is precisely what one finds in Deuteronomy 17:14-20. Interestingly, Psalm 1 begins by talking about what is *not* considered appropriate behavior for people. The blessed, or happy, person is one who "does not walk by the advice of the wicked, or in the way of sinners does not stand, and in the seat of scorners does not sit" (Ps 1:1). Similarly, Deuteronomy 17:14-20 begins by identifying what kings are *not* supposed to do. The king is not to be a foreigner, is not acquire a great number of horses (i.e., amass a large standing army), is not to return Israel to slavery, is not to acquire a large number of wives, and is not to amass great wealth (vv. 14-18). Next, Psalm 1 and Deuteronomy 17 proceed to identify what is expected: in both cases the primary demand is to "read" Torah. In Psalm 1, Torah is to be the object of the psalmist's delight *(ḥpṣ)* and meditation *(hgh)*. In Deuteronomy 17, the king is to have in his possession "a copy of this Torah" (i.e., apparently the Deuteronomic law), which he is to "read *(qrʾ)* all the days of his life in order that he will learn to fear YHWH his God, [and] to observe all the ways of this Torah and to do these statutes" (v. 19).

Other considerations also draw these two psalms and Deuteronomy 17 together into an intertextual nexus. Although the diction is not identical, the stance of both psalmist and king is remarkably close. In Psalm 1 the righteous individual is one who "meditates" continually upon Torah.[25] The verb used here *(hgh)* need not refer to an act of silent reflection. In fact, there are numerous places where the tongue, or the mouth, stands as the subject of this particular verb. For example, Psalm 35:28 begins, "And my tongue shall tell *(hgh)* of your righteousness." Similarly, Psalm 71:24 affirms "Also my tongue, all day, shall tell of your righteousness." On the basis of these and other examples it has been argued that the form of meditation in the view of Psalm 1 is an audible murmuring of Torah.[26]

[25] The pairing of "day and night" in Psalm 1:2b is an example of merismus—the expression of a totality by means of contrasting parts. The temporal references are not to be taken as particular moments in time, but rather as an enduring whole.

[26] On this understanding, see Brownlee, "Psalms 1–2 as a Coronation Liturgy," 323. Also see Hans-Joachim Kraus, *Psalms 1–59: A Commentary,* trans. Hilton C. Oswald (Minneapolis: Augsburg, 1988) 117.

It is equally as important to note that the type of reading advocated by Deuteronomy 17 need not be understood as a silent act. In fact, one of the primary meanings of the verb *qr'*, is "to call" or even "to shout." For example, the first human called the names of the animals that God brought (Gen 2:19). Perhaps even more telling, in Judges 7:3 Gideon is commanded to "Call out in the hearing of the people"—an act that would have required significant use of the voice. Similarly, in Judges 9:7 the narrator reports that Jothan "went and stood on the top of Mt. Gerizim, and he lifted his voice and called. . . ." This is clearly an act of shouting. The point, then, is that the act of "reading" that the king is to engage in "all the days of his life" can easily connote an oral reading similar to the meditation described in Psalm 1.[27]

In spite of the connections that I have described, it can be argued that the strongest basis for reading Psalm 1 in relation to Deuteronomy 17 is the first psalm's connection to Psalm 2. After all, Psalm 1 doesn't specifically mention a king. But there is another possibility for relating Psalm 1 to Deuteronomy 17:14-20. Miller has suggested that the picture of the king in Deuteronomy 17 is framed to present the king as "the model Israelite."[28] The king is not to be above the law, but is a servant of YHWH and a student of Torah. Admittedly there is something of an idealistic yearning in these restrictions, because Israel's kings rarely lived up to the requirements (a fact of which Deuteronomy is quite aware). Nonetheless, this "democratizing tendency" of Deuteronomy draws the faithful king in Deuteronomy 17 and the righteous individual of Psalm 1 much closer together than has sometimes been seen.[29]

So far, the quest to determine answers to the ambiguities in Psalms 1 and 2 (i.e., Which Torah? Which king?) has led to Deuteronomy 17:14-20 via thematic and intertextual connections. We might tentatively fill in any gaps presented in the Psalter's opening psalms by saying that Torah *includes* the Deuteronomic instruction and the king is the one who is con-

---

[27] It is also worth noting that the duration of the king's reading in Deuteronomy 17:19 is "all the days of his life." While not an example of merismus, the use of the word "day" *(yom)* in both Deuteronomy 17:19 and Psalm 1:2, along with the hyperbolic rhetoric in both instances, provides a further connection between the two texts.

[28] Miller, *Deuteronomy*, 149.

[29] Miller uses the expression "democratizing tendency" in his discussion. *Deuteronomy*, 148.

tinually faithful to that instruction. Heard this way, the psalms direct us to the emergence of kingship in Israel's life. From its canonical (boundary) location Deuteronomy looks forward to the appearance of monarchy. What is more, it holds out possibilities for the institution. It *can* be good. A king who is not self-interested, who is subservient to YHWH, and who adheres diligently to Torah can be a good king.

At the same time, Deuteronomy is not naïve about the institution of monarchy. It is introduced as a concession to Israel's request to be "like all the nations which are around me" (17:14). Given Deuteronomy's disposition toward other nations (e.g., Deut 7; 9:4; 12:29-32; 20; et al), this is no neutral request by Israel! To the request, YHWH makes an emphatic response,[30] "you shall surely place over you a king which YHWH your God will choose" (17:15). YHWH's emphatic comment should not be taken as divine enthusiasm. Its tone is more like, "You're going to do what you want to do, *but* here are the guidelines if I'm going to have anything to do with it."

It is important to remember that boundaries exist between entities. Heard strictly from within the bounds of the Book of Deuteronomy the "this Torah" of Deuteronomy 17:18 almost certainly refers solely to Deuteronomy.[31] But as a part of the larger canon, Deuteronomy "summarizes and brings to an end the beginning period of Israel's history, the story of redemption and the formation of a people instructed by the Lord."[32] These are, after all, "the words that *Moses* spoke to all Israel" (Deut 1:1). This is the same Moses who mediated the divine gift of Torah at Sinai. Even though a generation and a wilderness stand between Sinai and the plains of Moab, a reader who has followed the story of Israel's emergence and who stands with the new generation being instructed by Moses east of the Jordan would find it hard to bracket out earlier words of instruction. And so, at this boundary moment in Israel's life, the reader stands in a period where YHWH and YHWH's Torah are still the authoritative guides for life; but, the reader looks forward to a time when YHWH

[30] The NRSV begins the translation of v. 15 with "you may indeed set . . . ." The Hebrew syntax features an infinitive absolute followed by the finite form of the same verb. Literally the construction may be read, "Placing you shall place." It is an emphatic structure that carries a force somewhat difficult to render into the English.

[31] A.D.H. Mayes, *Deuteronomy,* The New Century Bible Commentary (Grand Rapids: Eerdmans, 1981) 273.

[32] Miller, *Deuteronomy,* 9.

will acquiesce to kingship *if* that king will submit to YHWH and Torah. At the boundary, Israel can sense alternatives. One can live by YHWH and Torah alone. Or one can attempt to live by YHWH, Torah, *and* King. From the evaluative point of view of Deuteronomy, one has a hunch that the better choice would be to forgo the adventure with kingship.[33] But such was not to be for Israel.

Expanding the Conversation: Psalms 1, 2, and the Books of Samuel

The argument so far has been that the dual focus upon Torah and kingship that opens the Psalter leads us to consider certain moments of emergence in Israel's life. In the quest to answer the question, "Which Torah, and which king?" posed by Psalms 1 and 2, thematic and intertextual clues directed us to Deuteronomy 17:14-20. There YHWH and Torah still rule, but kingship is also envisioned. The final shape of the canon would have us understand that there were deep tensions between the notions of YHWH's rule and the earthly monarch's rule embedded in Israel's earliest premonitions of monarchy. Alternatives typically create tensions and more often than not life is lived between competing claims. Such was Israel's destiny.

The same questions that directed us to Deuteronomy invite us to consider the time when monarchy actually emerged as a political institution in Israel. This, of course, occurs in the Books of Samuel. There, the tensions between Torah, YHWH, and a human king suggested by Psalms 1 and 2 and envisioned by Deuteronomy, come into full play.

Interlude

Deuteronomy 17:14-20, to the extent that it looks forward from its canonical position, clearly has in mind the emergence of monarchy that is narrated in the stories of Samuel. However, the intervening books contain the first rumblings that eventuate in the monarchic experiment.[34] It is useful to comment upon a few features of this "interlude."

---

[33] On "evaluative point of view" see Powell, *What Is Narrative Criticism?*, 23–25.

[34] The Books of Joshua, Judges, 1 and 2 Samuel (along with 1 and 2 Kings) contain many points of contact with the theology of the Book of Deuteronomy. Traditionally referred to as the "Former Prophets," critical scholars normally use the designation "Deu-

Israel's road to monarchy was a ponderous one. The literature that recounts this journey reflects increasing tensions between notions of YHWH's rule and earthly kingship. Early in the story Joshua can exclaim, "Cry out, because YHWH has given the city to you" (Josh 6:16)! The text does not hide the fact that more than a little human effort is involved in the taking of Jericho, but from the point of view of Joshua, the victory is God's. The same claim is made in Joshua 24:12-13 when Joshua claims, "Not by your sword or by your bow, but I [i.e., YHWH] gave to you a land on which you had not toiled . . . ." To even the casual reader of the Book of Joshua it is quite clear that swords and bows have been more than a little instrumental in Israel's emergence in the land. Still, human accomplishments seem visibly subordinated to divine performance in the Book of Joshua.

The Book of Judges carries forward a similar claim in its refrain that "the Spirit of YHWH came" upon particular judges (e.g., Judg 3:10; 6:34; 11:29; 14:6). But it is much more of a tortured and tensive claim than the affirmations in Joshua. Judges 3:15-30 goes to great length to chronicle the shrewdness of the left-handed Ehud. The cunning of Jael spares Israel from the Canaanites (Judg 4:17-22). Jephthah, not content with the gift of YHWH's spirit, makes a rash vow that results in the death of his daughter (Judg 11:29-40). Samson disobeys his parents' wishes and cavorts with foreign women and prostitutes (Judg 13–16). To be sure, each of these stories of deliverance understands God to have been involved (e.g., 3:28; 4:23; 11:29; 16:28). However, the human capacity for leadership—with all of its strengths and weaknesses—seems more visibly present along side divine leadership than had been the case in the Joshua material. There YHWH had entered into the fray by throwing down giant hailstones and by causing the sun to stand still (Josh 10:11-14). In Judges, the victory goes to people whose acts of shrewdness, deception, and whose questionable characteristics are described in considerable detail.

Perhaps one of the most telling texts is found in the story of Gideon. After a successful military engagement against the Midianites, the Israelites ask Gideon to "rule" over them. Gideon replies that neither he nor his son will rule over the people, but rather that YHWH will rule (Judg 8:22-35).

---

teronomistic History" when speaking of these books to underscore the influence of Deuteronomic theology in their shaping.

The verb used in this exchange is *māšhal* ("to rule," "to have dominion") and not the verb *mālak* ("to be king"). But regardless of the word used, the text would have us understand that Gideon senses the request to be a shift from divine to human leadership. That he includes his son in the refusal may also be a rejection of any form of dynastic rule.

Ironically, Gideon's son Abimelech does make an attempt to rule over Israel. In fact, Joshua 9:6 acknowledges that a group of influential Israelites gather at Shechem where they, literally, "kinged Abimelech as a king" (i.e., made him king). It was, however, an aborted attempt. In a scene that hauntingly foreshadows the later demise of Saul, God sends an evil spirit that causes friction between Abimelech and his supporters (9:23). In the end, Abimelech dies.

It is interesting to note that Abimelech, Jephthath, and Samson share a similar character trait. Abimelech is the child of Gideon through a concubine. Jephthath is Gilead's son through a prostitute. Samson frolics in the arms of prostitutes and Philistine women. In the end, Abimelech is killed; Jephthah's daughter is sacrificed because of his foolish vow; and Samson is blinded by the Philistines only to die with them in his final act of vengeance. Might the implied author be hinting that a shroud of "otherness," of "like the nations," hovers about these less than stellar characters? Such a possibility is in bounds, given the nationalistic tenor of Deuteronomic theology.

As the Book of Judges draws to a close, the reader encounters a series of bizarre incidents punctuated with the remark "In those days there was no king in Israel" (18:1; 19:1; 21:25). The narrator would have us to understand that in order to prevent violence, murder, and mayhem, a king is necessary. Unqualified affirmation in divine leadership alone has become a problematic platform. But, unqualified affirmation in human leadership as experienced in the closing chapters of Judges has become equally as problematic. Among the alternatives possible for Israel, kingship seems increasingly viable.

In the Book of Ruth, which follows Judges in Christian Bibles,[35] the activity of God is relatively subdued. Through the sometimes shrewd, risky, and determined actions of the various characters, the story makes

[35] Christian Bibles reflect the Greek Bible's (Septuagint) order here. The Hebrew Bible locates the Book of Ruth among the Writings—the third division of the Hebrew Bible.

its way from hunger and death to food and life. The child that is born to Ruth and Boaz at the end of the story is the grandfather of David. The way has been paved for monarchy in Israel.[36] That story is narrated in the Books of Samuel.

A King Like All the Nations

Psalm 2 is frequently, and appropriately, read against the backdrop of 2 Samuel 7—Nathan's oracle of a Davidic dynasty.[37] However, in light of the preceding discussion that has read Psalms 1 and 2 in association with Deuteronomy 17, I would suggest that there is another text in Samuel that should be considered, i.e., 1 Samuel 8. The request of the people in 1 Samuel 8:5 is for the aging leader to *"place over us a king to judge us like all the nations."* The language is more than a little evocative of Deuteronomy 17:14 where the people announce, "I will *place over me a king like all the nations."* In addition to identical language (see the highlights), Samuel's scathing critique of monarchy portrays the king as one who will do exactly what Deuteronomy 17:15-20 forbids! Nowhere in Samuel's enumeration of kingly actions that the people can expect is the reading of Torah—the very thing that Deuteronomy 17 requires! But Samuel's words fall on deaf ears and the people round out the episode by saying, "No, but there will be a *king over us.* Also we, we will be *like all the nations.* And our king will judge us, and go out before us and fight our battles" (1 Sam 8:19b-20).

---

[36] If it is possible that the "like the nations" character that hovered about Abimelech, Jephthath, and Samson led to their demise, a reader might wonder if any descendent of the union between a Moabite and an Israelite will fare much better. Fatal flaws have a way of turning up! (On the suspicions aroused by foreigners in the Book of Ruth, see Danna Nolan Fewell and David Miller Gunn, *Compromising Redemption: Relating Characters in the Book of Ruth*, Literary Currents in Biblical Interpretation [Louisville: Westminster/John Knox, 1990].) In fact, Kirsten Nielsen has argued that the Book of Ruth functions as an apologetic for the well known fact that David had a mixed ancestry. Since this question-able detail about David's background could not be hidden, it was important to give it the best "spin" possible. The Book of Ruth certainly serves this function (Nielsen, *Ruth: A Commentary*, OTL (Louisville: Westminster/John Knox, 1997). The fatal flaw might still be hidden deep in David, but the story of Ruth has reduced its ominous character.

[37] For example, Kraus, *Psalms 1–59*, 131–32; James L. Mays, *Psalms*, Interpretation (Louisville: Westminster/John Knox, 1994) 47; McCann, "The Book of Psalms," 689.

Now the relationship between Psalm 1/2 and Deuteronomy 17 that already has been sketched would be sufficient grounds to hear 1 Samuel 8 in conjunction with the two psalms. But there are other compelling connections.

Key vocabulary of Israel's request in 1 Samuel 8 is found in Psalm 2. In 1 Samuel the people desire a king *(mlk)* like the nations *(gym)*, who will judge or rule *(špt)* over them. Samuel, as YHWH's spokesman, thinks the request is a bad idea. Psalm 2 speaks of the nations *(gym*—vv. 1, 8) who have kings *(mlk*—vv. 2, 10) and judges/rulers *(špt*—v. 10). What the people request in 1 Samuel 8 is very much the subject matter of Psalm 2.

Furthermore, Samuel's negative evaluation of the request for a king like the nations is shared by Psalm 2. In the psalm, the nations "meditate" *(hgh*—v. 1) on inappropriate matters and their kings are in rebellion against YHWH and the one YHWH has selected. The point of the view of the psalm is that a king like those of the nations is not what Israel should want. In contrast to these, Israel's king is installed *(nsk)* by YHWH (Ps 2:6). The only other place in the Hebrew Bible where this verb is used with the meaning of "install" or "set" is Proverbs 8:23. There, Wisdom has been "set" or "installed" by YHWH at the beginning of creation. In both cases, then, YHWH is the one who sets. This is at odds with the request of the people, who desire that Samuel "set" *(śîm)* a king over them.[38] So, vocabulary and similar viewpoints about kings of the nations invite the introduction of the Psalter to be heard in association with the emergence of kingship in 1 Samuel 8.

Amazingly, the pejorative view of kingship offered in 1 Samuel 8 is followed by a strikingly positive portrayal in the following chapter and a half (9:1–10:16). Specifically, in 9:16 YHWH reveals to Samuel that, on the following day, he is to anoint a Benjaminite who will "save my people from the hand of the Philistines, because I have seen the [suffering][39] of

---

[38] Interestingly, in Deuteronomy 17 YHWH acknowledges that the people will set or place *(śîm)* a king over themselves. The people are the subject of the verb. However, Deuteronomy makes it clear that the one they place over themselves is to be chosen *(bāḥar)* by God. Although the diction is different, the claim is similar to that of Psalm 2. There are kings (of the nations) and then there are kings (of YHWH's choice and installation)! There is some built in tension here, then. There are potentially "good" kings and potentially "bad" kings. This potential to slide either way will be a large issue as monarchy becomes a socio-political reality in Israel.

[39] The MT lacks "suffering" and reads merely ". . . because I have seen my people . . . ." On the basis of the Greek and the Aramaic the word *ʿanî* ("suffering") has been supplied.

my people, because their cry has come to me."[40] The language is amazingly reminiscent of God's address to Moses in Exodus 3:7: "I have indeed seen the affliction of my people who are in Egypt, and their cry I have heard because of their taskmasters, because I know their pain." Astonishingly, Israel's first king is compared to Moses! Once Saul is anointed Samuel instructs him that he is to "save [Israel] from the enemies round about."[41] As Walter Brueggemann has observed, here the "act of kingmaking is soteriological. Saul is to save. The act is also ecclesiological. It is for the sake of community. Saul is to save and to make this community freshly possible."[42] I will return to these points later.

Just as Psalm 2 shared intertextual connections with 1 Samuel 8, there are also connections with 1 Samuel 9:1–10:16. Psalm 2:2 lauds YHWH's *mĕšîaḥ* ("anointed"), while 1 Samuel 10:1 narrates that Samuel "anointed" *(mšḥ)* Saul. Brueggemann perceptibly notes that the anointing of Saul is not for the sake of monarchy, but rather for *ʿamî*, "my people," who are mentioned three times in 1 Samuel 9:16-17.[43] Kingship is for the people, and not the people for kingship. Interestingly, Psalm 2 speaks not of my people but of "my king" *(malkî)* and "my son" *(benî)*. When read intertextually, the purpose of YHWH's anointed king and begotten child in Psalm 2 is for the well-being of YHWH's people in 1 Samuel 9. So, in the view of Psalm 2 and 1 Samuel 8, a king like the nations is anathema. But in view of Psalm 2 and 1 Samuel 9:1–10:16 (and also Deut 17), a king that YHWH chooses is a potential savior for Israel.

Now the remarkably positive evaluation of kingship is difficult to miss when 1 Samuel 8 and 9:1–10:16 are read together. To be sure, one might argue that the latter text has in view an institution other than a full-blown monarchy. The word that is typically used to describe Saul in

---

[40] This scene is a classic example of *analepsis* where an event that has actually occurred earlier is narrated later (see Powell, *What Is Narrative Criticism?*, 37). The rhetorical force of this literary device is to stress that the encounter between Samuel and Saul is to be seen as providential and that the events that transpire should be regarded as divinely approved. This all the more highlights the contrast between 1 Samuel 8 and 9:1–10:16.

[41] This instruction is not found in the MT but is supplied on the basis of the Greek and the Latin.

[42] Walter Brueggemann, *First and Second Samuel*, Interpretation (Louisville: Westminster/John Knox, 1990) 74.

[43] Brueggemann, *First and Second Samuel*, 72.

9:1–10:16 is not *mĕlĕk* ("king"), but *nāgîd* ("leader," "ruler," "prince"— e.g., 9:16; 10:1). The negative force of chapter 8 was directed against the former, and the subsequent panel beginning at 10:17 will rail against the people's desire for a *mĕlĕk*/king. Also, Saul's single function in 9:1-10:16 is to save the people. Perhaps this unit, then, envisions and blesses a particular form of limited monarchy. If this is the case, the implied author could be a little more explicit. So, what is one to make of this "bipolar" view of kingship found in 1 Samuel?

In the first half of the twentieth century source critics used to explain the tension by positing at least two sources. One was in favor of monarchy, the other was opposed. Although the dating of sources has always been hazardous, it was usually agreed that the promonarchial source was earlier than the antimonarchial—the latter which reflected life under the actual existence of overreaching monarchs. This may indeed be exactly the case. However, the two views come to us interwoven in the whole of the Samuel material. So how is the reader to take the narrative as it currently stands?

Brevard Childs has offered a helpful solution. Building on the work of source critics (especially Julius Wellhausen) Childs sketches the arrangement of the promonarchial material (source A) and the antimonarchial material (source B) like this:

B—8:1-22
A—9:10-16
B—10:17-27
A—11:1-15
B—12:1-25

Childs observes that both traditions are present. Neither is completely eliminated in favor of the other. Kings may be bad, but kings may be good; both possibilities exist. The two positions are not merely juxtaposed, though. They are strategically crafted so that the antimonarchial view has the preeminent position, surrounding and standing in the center of the promonarchial texts. There is a clear bias in the final shape of the material. However, both positions exist as potential and viable alternatives for Israel's social and political organization.[44]

---

[44] See Brevard Childs, *Introduction to the Old Testament as Scripture* (Philadelphia: Fortress, 1979) 277–78.

Childs' argument concerns theological considerations that may be drawn on the basis of the final shape of the text, and that is important. But to hear these competing voices from within the conversational character of a story is to hear a lively debate about divergent possibilities. There is a dynamic character to this discussion that is not finally settled—at least once and for all. And while it is not the purpose of this study to explore and describe the ancient social world using all of the tools available to historians, the truth of the matter is that these divergent views on monarchy likely represented the sentiments of the people from the beginning. Source critical notions of an early source and a late source, the first favorable and the latter antipathetic toward monarchy, are too simplistic. Just as the narrative reflects, both views were almost certainly present from the earliest moments that monarchy appeared upon Israel's radar screen.

Preliminary Observations

The discussion to this point has shown that there are ambiguities within Psalms 1 and 2, that there are ambiguities when the two psalms are read together, and that there are ambiguities when the psalms are read along with other psalms. In an effort to respond to these ambiguities, the content of Psalms 1 and 2 led us to consider intertextual connections with Deuteronomy 17:14-20 and 1 Samuel 8–12. In these latter texts that debate the emergence of monarchy in Israel, the people stand at the threshold between two eras. With one foot still planted in the era of YHWH and Torah alone, Israel stretches the other foot toward human kingship. Even as that foot drops, there is a reluctance to move a step farther. Questions linger and gnaw. Can the old traditions that have served so well be carried forward? Will the new form of social organization completely eradicate the claims of old faith, or at the least, distort them until they are no longer recognizable? Or is it possible that the old claims can viably coexist with human kings, to instruct and nurture them?

There is no definitive answer, because Deuteronomy 17, 1 Samuel 8–12, and Psalms 1/2 leave intact both the possibility and the peril of the peculiar mix of YHWH, Torah, and human kingship. The text will not eliminate the alternatives. But the intertextual reading does suggest that there are at least two guides for defining the wholesomeness of the mix.

First, kings and Israel—together—are to read Torah continually. One reading will not do. Both kings and people must realize that society is not static and that old readings of Torah will not necessarily suffice in changed circumstances. The passing of time will call for new readings, new interpretations, new negotiations.

Second, this collage of texts underscores the fundamental purpose of kingship—indeed, of any new form of social organization that Israel will ever consider. From YHWH's perspective, the purpose of "my king" (read also, *any* form of social organization), is "to save" "my people." To return to Brueggemann's remarks, any notion of soteriology or ecclesiology that does less is bankrupt from the start.[45]

Canon and Congregation

In this section I will attempt to make connections between the concept of canon in general, the canonical texts that have been discussed, and the life of congregations. While my remarks will be informed by, and interact with, social-scientific studies of congregations, I am more interested in the theological underpinnings of congregational life.[46] After all, the explicit and tacit theological convictions of congregations are what most noticeably set them apart from other benevolent and humanitarian institutions. The connections that I draw will not constitute a program to strengthen congregational identity, or an instrument to study congregational culture—although they may prove helpful to people who seek to introduce such programs or design such instruments. Perhaps they will

---

[45] Brueggemann, *First and Second Samuel*, 74.

[46] In making this statement I do not mean to imply that a congregation's theology exists in a vacuum. Indeed, one might learn far more about a congregation's theology by focusing upon and describing the implicit theology of its budget than by studying its mission statement—if it even has the latter (and it will almost certainly have the former). However, rather than approach congregations through the frames of resources, ecology, process, or leadership, I am more interested in a congregation's culture, or identity (on these "frames" see Nancy Ammerman, et al., *Studying Congregations: A New Handbook* [Nashville: Abingdon, 1998]). It is the theological identity/culture of a congregation that leads to examining leadership and resources, for example, through a theological lens—something that would not likely occur (for better or worse!) to a Fortune 500 corporation. My focus primarily upon theology and culture, then, reflects my interest and should not be taken as a value judgment upon other possible frames for congregational study.

be most useful to congregations that are attempting to articulate and embody a vision that is faithful to the larger tradition and that is aware of the unique and dynamic ecology in which the congregation is located.

The conversations among Psalms 1 and 2, Deuteronomy 17, and 1 Samuel 8–12 come to Christians and Jews as part of the canon of Scripture. As such, they exert influence and make certain claims upon the faith and practice of those of us within the Judeo-Christian tradition. To return to James Sanders's observation, canon answers two fundamental questions: "who am I, or we, and what are we to do?"[47] The foundational nature of canon and these canonical questions are a major element of the "larger tradition" that every congregation will inescapably inherit.[48] Or, we might draw on the insights of Clifford Geertz and say that canon is very much a part of the worldview (the "comprehensive, factual 'is'") that gives rise to the ethos ("the powerfully coercive 'ought'") of any given congregation.[49] In myriad and complex ways, canon is constitutive of congregational culture.

This is not to say, of course, that canon *alone* gives rise to a congregation's culture. First United Methodist Church downtown quite likely will have a very different identity/culture from Mt. Zion United Methodist Church that is part of a rural, three point charge. Members' ages, occupations, education, ethnicity, political leanings; the age of the churches; the presence of a pipe organ or a weathered piano; whether or not there are church-owned cemeteries and who's buried (and who *may be* buried) in them; lined asphalt parking lot or gravel drive—these and hosts of other factors all are a part of the variable mix of "genes" that will contribute to the unique identity of a congregation.[50] While the parking lot may not be

---

[47] James Sanders, "Adaptable for Life," in *From Sacred Story to Sacred Text* (Philadelphia: Fortress, 1987) 17.

[48] On "larger tradition" and a specific congregation's relationship to it, see Nancy T. Ammerman, "Culture and Identity in the Congregation," in *Studying Congregations,* 78–81.

[49] Clifford Geertz, "Ethos, World View, and the Analysis of Sacred Symbols," in *The Interpretation of Cultures* (New York: Basic Books, 1973) 126.

[50] Numbers of studies have described the uniqueness of various congregations that all have the larger Christian tradition (and its canon) in view, yet order their lives quite differently from one another. Perhaps the classic discussion is offered by James Hopewell in *Congregation: Stories and Structures* (Philadelphia: Fortress, 1987). Drawing upon the narrative distinctions of Northrop Frye, Hopewell describes four congregational worldviews: canonic, empiric, gnostic, and charismatic. For a different schema, see the five congregational self-images proposed by Carl S. Dudley and Sally A. Johnson, "Congregational

directly connected to the organ, each will have to connect to canon if it is to be a *church* parking lot, or a *church* organ—otherwise, we might just as well be talking about the lot and organ at a baseball stadium!

With these comments in mind, I would like to recall the two guides for sorting out the different claims about the emergence of monarchy in Israel. Israel's kings and people were to read Torah continually, and the purpose of monarchy (indeed, any form of social organization) was to save God's people. I now bring those guides into a discussion of canon, culture, and ecology.

The continual reading of Torah and the act of saving "my people" bring the trinity of canon, culture, and ecology together into this dynamic configuration:

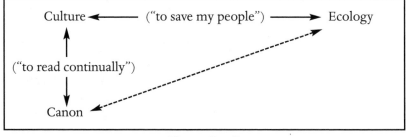

Figure One[51]

In Figure One, congregational culture is informed by a continual reading of canon/Scripture. But because it is the nature of canon to exhibit a "Yes, but . . ." character (e.g., YHWH reigns, *but* human monarchs reign), the canon must be constantly scrutinized to ascertain the Word of God because one reading will not suffice. James Sanders writes that the Bible

is a highly pluralistic document. Hence, no tyranny can be established on its basis, for there is always something in it to challenge whatever is con-

Self-Images for Social Ministry," in Carl S. Dudley, Jackson W. Carroll, and James P. Wind, eds., *Carriers of Faith* (Louisville: Westminster/John Knox, 1991) 104–21.

[51] This diagram is an adaptation of the triangle used by James Sanders to describe the canonical process. See Sanders, *Canon and Community: a Guide to Canonical Criticism,* Guides to Biblical Scholarship (Philadelphia: Fortress, 1984) 77–78.

structed on it. Its full context is very broad and very wide and sponsors serious dialogue. No single program, political, social, economic, or otherwise can escape the challenge of something in it.[52]

The solid, bidirectional arrow signifies this dynamic interaction between canon and culture.

At the same time, the congregation's culture is dynamically and intimately related to the ecology in which it finds itself (signified by the solid, bidirectional arrow). The relationship between the two is not exactly "us versus them." The boundary between the two is somewhat permeable. As the editors of *Studying Congregations: A New Handbook* observe, "A congregation can affect its environment as the congregation engages in outreach activity . . . but it is also shaped by the people and resources and other institutions in that environment."[53] However, just as the rationale of the congregation's existence (along with its processes, leadership, and resources) is theological, so to is its ethos: "to save my people."

The relationship between ecology and canon is less intimate (hence, the broken line), but nonetheless there can be a dynamic interface between the two. This might be described as a form of public or civil religion that does touch base with Scripture as needed but is not formally connected with a particular ecclesiological body. Some examples might include Habitat for Community, the Christian Coalition, Internet chat rooms, satellite broadcasts of religious services, etc. While the canon may not be a major source of identity for these parareligious groups, appeal may be made to certain portions of Scripture to legitimate their existence and actions.

It is important to note again the bidirectional flow of these relationships. For a congregation to embrace this dynamism means to remain open to the "yes, but . . ." character of canon, and to remain flexible in the event of ecological change. Negotiations among the vertexes of the triangle may be valid, but at best they are temporary. Thus construed, congregations are—to borrow Sanders's description of canon—both adaptable and stable.[54]

---

[52] Sanders, "Adaptable for Life," 30.

[53] Ammerman, et al., *Studying Congregations*, 14.

[54] Sanders, "Adaptable for Life."

For any congregation (whether new, established, or reemerging) that has undertaken the task to articulate and embody its mission/vision,[55] the process I have described can be helpful. For one thing, the focus is theological. Needs analyses, questionnaires, surveys, time lines, focus groups, census reports, and demographic studies (important as they may be) are not ends in themselves but tools in service of the congregation that is charged to care for God's people. For another thing, it underscores the dynamic associations among canon, culture, and ecology. Even a well-designed (and successfully embodied) vision statement will not eliminate these dynamics.[56] Failure to keep this awareness clearly in mind may lead to problems.

The following Figure represents a process that is stripped of its dynamic and interactive character and locked into a static loop.

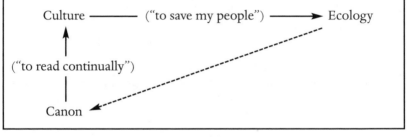

Figure Two

In Figure Two the lines are no longer bidirectional. Such a situation could exist in a congregation that perceives things to be going well. Challenges are few and what challenges exist are small and easily dealt with. Put simply, the world works and all is well. At its best, such a one directional flow may lead to inertia.[57] People see no reason to make changes

[55] Some students of congregations make a distinction between "mission" and "vision." They regard the former as identifying the basic purpose and identity of a congregation, and the latter as signifying the more pragmatic ways to live up to that purpose. See Jackson Carroll, "Leadership and the Study of the Congregation," in *Studying Congregations,* 179–80.

[56] On a "good" vision statement, see Carroll, "Leadership and the Study of Congregations," 183–84.

[57] On inertia, see Nancy Ammerman, *Congregation and Community* (New Brunswick, N.J.: Rutgers University Press, 1997) 63–64.

because congregational life seems to be functioning effectively and effi-
ciently. Of course, change for the sake of change is not desired. But when
a congregation's *openness to the possible need for change* is lost, its peripheral
vision is gone and it can see only what is straight ahead.

At its worst, the static loop that is sketched in Figure Two portrays a
situation open to ruthless manipulation. Dialogue is transformed to demand. Interaction is sacrificed on the altar of influence. Control replaces
compassion. Now, the same old reading of canon suffices to legitimate
the congregation. The congregation no longer listens to the world (ecology) but imposes its own agenda under the guise of good intentions. For
those in the world with the power to do so, the portions of canon that
best serve their own interests are advocated to the congregation. It is a
situation that favors those with power and a vested interest in the status
quo, a situation where might makes right, and a situation that will be taken
up more fully in the next chapter.

Summary

The beginning of Israel's story in the Book of Psalm raised the questions, "Which Torah and which king?" Intertextual clues led us to consider crucial moments in Israel's emergence as a people and a nation. The
first moment was when Israel stood on the threshold between the
wilderness and the land, guided by YHWH and Torah but with an eye directed toward human kingship in the future. The second moment was
when Israel actually embarked upon the monarchic experiment. At both
moments, alternatives hovered: YHWH/Torah alone? Human king?
YHWH/Torah and human king? Although the texts suggested the danger
in moving toward the hierarchical structure of monarchy, they also left
open the possibility that it might work if the king was a true student of
Torah and was concerned to save God's people.

As congregations overhear the story of Israel's emergence from a
wilderness band to a people ruled by a king, certain voices may be singled out:

- In moments of emergence there are always alternatives. For Israel,
  the choices are both theological and sociological.

- Moments of emergence involve the struggle to bring old traditions into the present and the future.

- ⟡ For Israel, the choice between alternatives is guided by constant interaction with Torah/canon and out of a concern for the well-being of God's people.

- ⟡ In a healthy situation, there is a dynamic relationship among canon, culture, and ecology.

- ⟡ A static situation exhibits inertia. The vision of a previous generation is assumed to be valid for all time. Those who benefit from the status quo will resist change. A singular reading of the text, even if it brings harm to God's people, will suffice as long as it legitimizes the position of the individuals in power.

This story of emergence calls for congregations to be engaged in continual dialogue with Scripture, tradition, and context. It calls for openness to new visions, astonishing discoveries, and wholesome change. It calls for congregations to remember that they are God's people entrusted with the vocation of caring for the rest of God's people.

3

Establishment

espite the suspicion of many of the texts that narrate the story of monarchy's emergence in ancient Israel, the institution was probably inevitable. Anthony Ceresko has identified both external and internal factors that edged the tribal confederation toward monarchy.[1] While the Philistines pushed the confederation from the outside, disproportionate resources among the tribes and less than full tribal commitment to covenantal obligations exerted pressure from within. Consequently, monarchy emerged as the most viable alternative for Israel's survival in its contemporary context.

As we have seen, Israel's story in the Book of Psalms opens with monarchy in full bloom. To be sure, there are gaps in the opening that invite consideration of monarchy's emergence, and that was the subject of the previous chapter. But the force of the Psalter's beginning, and the pull of subsequent voices, will not let one linger too long and ponder premonarchic moments. Any ambiguities that remain about which Torah and which king will have to be settled on the basis of the conversations among the psalms that follow. To return to Meir Sternberg's remarks, we

---

[1] Anthony R. Ceresko, O.S.F.S., *Introduction to the Old Testament: A Liberation Perspective* (Maryknoll, N.Y.: Orbis, 1992) 125–36.

will no longer look to the past but will "look forward to new disclosures," to a "gradual release of clues" in order to settle unresolved issues.[2]

In this chapter I will describe Books One and Two of the Psalter (Psalms 1–72) as consisting of voices that affirm and challenge the established institution of monarchy in Israel. This important episode in Israel's story is narrated by psalms that, in various ways, propose and protest the monarchic adventure. As was the case in moments of emergence, neither voice is silenced. We will see that more voices protest the high claims of monarchy than sing its praises. But we will also see that the voices that propose monarchy are powerful indeed, and come at strategic places in the episode.

This narration of advocacy and dissent is intensely personal, social, and theological.[3] Conversations about such matters usually defy neat closure, and the ones that we will hear will be no different. But certain overtures can be made, at least provisionally, that might guide our listening to them and that might also be suggestive to congregations who recognize parts of their own narratives in the passionate voices of these psalms. That will be one of the goals of this chapter.

Conversations of Proposal and Protest

Voices of Proposal. On the whole, Books One and Two of the Psalter are keenly focused upon David. Of the seventy-two psalms in this collection, all but seventeen mention David in their superscriptions. Twelve of the thirteen psalms with superscriptions that associate the texts with events involving David in the Samuel stories are found in Psalms 1–72 (3, 7, 18, 34, 51, 52, 54, 56, 57, 59, 60, 63 [142 is the other such psalm]). In Israel's memory, David is the preeminent king of the past and the model for the ideal king of the present and future.[4] The connection between David and so many psalms in Books One and Two—however one chooses to under-

---

[2] Sternberg, *The Poetics of Biblical Narrative: Ideological Literature and the Drama of Reading* (Bloomington: Indiana University Press, 1985) 259.

[3] James L. Mays observes that Psalm 13 has these three dimensions (*Psalms*, Interpretation [Louisville: Westminster/John Knox, 1994] 78). At the risk of overreaching, it is tempting to claim the entire Psalter is much concerned about self, others, and God.

[4] On the ways that Israel remembered David, see Walter Brueggemann, *David's Truth in Israel's Imagination and Memory* (Philadelphia: Fortress, 1985).

stand this connection—imbues the collection with the aura of an established and highly regarded monarch. This in itself constitutes a rhetoric of proposal.

What is more, Royal Psalms (psalms about the king) bound the collection (Psalms 2 and 72), and punctuate the overall conversation in the first two books of the Psalter (Psalms 18, 20, 21, and 45).[5] Each of the voices is distinct in its proposal of monarchy, but each is unrelenting in its advocacy and the possibilities of the institution. If we allow the superscriptions and the canonical shaping of Psalms 1–72 to offer us guidance, the conversation in Books One and Two of the Psalter is intensely focused upon monarchy as an establishment worthy of legitimation and maintenance.

As a unit, the combined Psalms 1 and 2 initiate the monarchic proposal. The second half of this introductory unit, *Psalm 2*, received significant attention in the previous chapter, but a few features of the psalm deserve further comment. Verses 1-3 disclose a conspiracy of unnamed leaders and nations directed "against Yнwн and against his anointed *(měšîḥô)*." The verses may have in mind a particular historical event, but that event lies buried beneath the stealth of the psalm's diction. As it stands, "the language reflects primarily *all*—or *any*—nations that do not acknowledge the primacy of Israel's God, and therefore of Israel's king [emphasis added]."[6] While the claims of the psalm arise from the warp and woof of actual experience, the assertion that the "kings of *the earth*" are in rebellion against God and king reveals an understanding of reality that goes beyond mere historical reportage.

Verses 4-6 declare Yнwн's reaction to the conspiracy. The situation is laughable but not humorous, for Yнwн announces in anger, "I, I have set my king, upon Zion my holy mountain." The emphatic use of the personal pronoun underscores that the king rules only by virtue of divine deed. As a result of God's action, the king sits/rules in Zion like Yнwн sits/rules in heaven. Although Yнwн is the one who makes kings, God also gives the king actual power.

---

[5] On the placement of Royal Psalms in the canonical shaping of the Psalter, see Gerald Wilson, *The Editing of the Hebrew Psalter*, SBLDS (Chico, Calif.: Scholars Press, 1985) especially 207–8. Wilson's focus, though, is more on the Royal Psalms at the "seams" of the Book than upon the Royal Psalms that appear elsewhere.

[6] Peter C. Craigie, *Psalms 1–50*, Word Biblical Commentary (Waco: Word, 1983) 66.

In verses 7-9 the king speaks to relay the divine decree *(ḥōq)* that serves as the legitimation of his rule. The decree identifies the king as God's child: "My son are you; I, today, I have begotten you." The language, again, is emphatic: YHWH is the actor. The word "begotten" is clearly used metaphorically. The king becomes YHWH's begotten child "today," that is, already as a mature individual. But the force of this language should not be missed. Clearly, to speak of kingship is to speak of a socio-political institution. The psalm is forthright about that dimension of monarchy. But the psalm also portrays kingship in intimately personal and familial terms. The king and God relate as child and parent. Part of a familial relationship involves inheritance, and God grants nations of the world to the king. This grant involves actual power and the permission to use that power in stern ways.

Verses 10-12 admonish the earth's kings to submit wisely to YHWH, lest they incur divine anger—and, we might imagine, kingly anger as well! The concluding beatitude offers the positive warrant for serving YHWH: they (i.e., kings and nations) will be blessed, or happy.

Psalm 2 was likely used at the coronation or enthronement of a king, and is usefully interpreted in that context.[7] But as part of the introduction to Israel's story in the Book of Psalms, Psalm 2 offers an exceedingly high estimation of the institution of monarchy. Unlike the texts in Deuteronomy and 1 Samuel, here kingship is presented as God's choice. Gone is any trace of divine capitulation to human request. Instead, God "sets" and God "begets." God is parent, and king is child with all of the prerogatives of a favored child—especially power. The unanswered question at this point in the story is: How will the king use his power?

Although the psalm presents kingship and royal power as derivative (i.e., given by YHWH), the king is very much front and center. It is telling that in the rhetoric of Psalm 2, it is the king himself who announces the special status that he possesses as YHWH's child. Unlike the Gospels' announcements at Jesus' baptism and the transfiguration (e.g., Matt 3:17; 17:5), this announcement of sonship comes from the lips of the king instead of from heaven. There are more than a few clues then, that it would be reductionistic to read the psalm theologically without paying careful

---

[7] Craigie offers good discussion of the likely use of the psalm in a coronation ceremony (*Psalms 1–50*, 64–68).

attention to its ideological claims. The psalm serves as a powerful legitimation of monarchy in general, and given the presence of David in Psalms 1–72, the Davidic monarchy in particular.

A robust proposal for the establishment of monarchy is not limited to the beginning of Books One and Two. Hearty voices of advocacy follow. I choose to focus upon two particular points in the conversation. The first consists of the grouping of Psalms 18, 19, 20, and 21. The second is Psalm 45.

I find the juxtaposition of Psalms 18–21 intriguing. Here I will offer a few comments on each and its canonical location. *Psalm 18* is literarily complex, but it is generally listed among the Royal Psalms. More specifically, it has been called "a king's psalm of thanksgiving."[8] The superscription of the psalm that speaks both of distress and deliverance of the king is somewhat indicative of its content, although it is of no use in identifying the exact event that gave rise to the song.[9] One might think of the psalm in this way: verses 1-6 present the situation of distress and a call for help; verses 7-19 describe a theophany and God's act of deliverance; verses 20-30 contain a rationale for God's deliverance; verses 31-50 describe God's benefits to the king and the king's response.[10]

At the outset, things seem bleak for the king. Indeed, this beginning hardly sounds like the monarchic proposal that was heard in Psalm 2. Here, monarchy seems more in jeopardy than settled. However, God responds to the king's cry and comes in such a way that all of creation is thrown into convulsion.[11] The natural world announces the arrival of YHWH who rescues the king from danger.

The rationale offered by the king to explain his deliverance may sound excessive and self-laudatory, but perhaps is best heard in association with

---

[8] See Craigie, *Psalms 1–50*, 171. Kraus proposes a similar designation (Hans-Joachim Kraus, *Psalms 1–59: A Commentary*, trans. Hilton C. Oswald (Minneapolis: Augsburg, 1988) 257.

[9] See the parallel version in 2 Samuel 22. The same introduction occurs there and seems somewhat jarring because Saul was killed much earlier in the narrator's story. This, along with the broad designation of "enemies" gives the psalm, even in its narrative setting, the feel of a reasonably open and loose song of thanksgiving that would make it an appropriate response to deliverance from any battle.

[10] For another possibility, see Kraus, *Psalms 1–59*, 258–65.

[11] For comparable theophanic texts see Judges 5:4-5; Psalm 29; Micah 1:3-4; and to a lesser degree, Amos 1:2.

entrance, or Torah liturgies, like Psalms 15 and 24.[12] Both psalms articulate qualifications for entering the Temple's precincts. Among other things, Psalm 15:2 insists that one should walk blamelessly *(tāmîm)* and do righteousness *(ṣedek)*. Psalm 24:4 maintains that one who would approach the Temple should possess clean hands. These, along with other qualifications to approach the divine presence should not be taken as exclusionary. Rather, in the best sense of Torah they stake out in broad claims the character that befits one who would dare worship God. They instruct and hold before the worshiping community the lifestyle that God desires in all of life. So, in Psalm 18:23 (and verse 26 by implication) the king affirms that he has been blameless *(tāmîm)*, and in verses 20 and 24 he underscores that he has been righteous *(ṣdk)*. Also, verses 20 and 24 speak of the king's "clean hands." The Hebrew words are different from those in Psalm 24, but the meaning seems to be essentially the same. The king, then, is claiming that he has been one who has given himself over to God's instruction. In fact, he acknowledges that the Torah encountered in worship has been before him daily ("ordinances" and "statutes"—verse 23). The encounter of the Holy God and the king described in Psalm 18 is possible because of the king's Torah fidelity.[13]

Verses 31-50 offer a long list of benefits (here, battle skills) provided by YHWH. Verses 43-45, with their language of "nations" and "people" from whom the king is delivered, are highly evocative of Psalm 2 where God promises the anointed king victory over people and nations. If the beginning of Psalm 18 seemed to call into question the bold proposal for kingship of Psalm 2, the developments within the former psalm tend actually to reinforce the second psalm's claims. God "will do steadfastness to his anointed, to David and to his descendants forever" (v. 50).

The literary structure of *Psalm 19* is easier to describe than that of Psalm 18. It consists of two basic sections. Verses 1-6 reflect upon nature's testimony to God, and verses 7-14 ponder the knowledge of YHWH that is available through Torah. However, the precise nature of the relationship between the two sections is every bit as complicated as the thorniest interpretive issues in Psalm 18. Here I can only suggest some possibilities for hearing the psalm and acknowledge that there are other legitimate stances.

---

[12] On the designations of entrance/Torah liturgies, see Kraus, *Psalms 1–59*, 226, 311.

[13] Once again, one thinks of Deuteronomy 17 and its demand for the king to read Torah all of his life.

First, there are a number of "hooks" that invite hearing Psalms 18 and 19 together. In Psalm 18, the shaking earth and the stormy skies announce the presence of God who comes to save. In Psalm 19, the rhythmic movement of the sun across the sky day after day mysteriously conveys insights about God. In Psalm 18:30, the way of God is perfect *(tāmîm)* and in 19:7 the Torah of YHWH is perfect *(tĕmîmâ)*. Similarly, in 18:23 the king—aided by Torah—was blameless *(tāmîm),* and in 19:13 the one who keeps Torah—aided by YHWH—will be blameless *('êtām).* The Torah piety that characterized the king in 18:20-24 is advocated to everyone in 19:7-14. In addition to these thematic and lexical associations, the juxtaposition of Torah and kingship that opened the Psalter (Pss 1 and 2) invites hearing Psalms 18 and 19 together.[14] This will also be the case as we move to Psalm 20—a psalm that asks God's help for the king—and Psalm 21—a psalm in which the king offers thanks for God's help. At the very center of this cluster of psalms that petition God to help the king, followed by the king's thanksgiving, stands the mysterious, life-giving force of Torah.

Psalm 19:1-6 meditates upon the astonishing insight that the heavens, and especially the sun, speak of God.[15] It is a mysterious speech because there are no words that one might hear. Nevertheless, for this psalmist the voice is as perceptible as the beauty of the sun and the shadows that change throughout the day. To glimpse this beauty is to glimpse also a stance toward God and God's creation.

No less beautiful and mysterious is God's Torah (vv. 7-14). It is a source of knowledge, joy, reverence, and calls for continual reflection. Torah is not simply a code of ethics. Perhaps more importantly, it is an

---

[14] James L. Mays has also noted that reading Psalms 18 and 19 (as well as 118 and 119) in association may be profitable. He questions, "Is it a mere accident that both [i.e. Pss 19 and 119], with their emphasis on torah as the center of life, follow a psalm in which, as in Psalm 2, the problem is the nations against whom the Lord acts to save the righteous one as a vindication of his sovereignty?" Rather than read the connections in the context of Israel's story in the psalms, he suggests the connections were understood eschatologically by the post-exilic community yearning for God's redemption. See James L. Mays, "The Place of the Torah-Psalms in the Psalter," *JBL* 106 (March 1987) 3–13; see especially 11.

[15] Upon the meditative qualities of Psalm 19, see Walter Harrelson, "Psalm 19: A Meditation on God's Glory in the Heavens and in God's Law," in M. Patrick Graham, Rick R. Marrs, and Steven L. McKenzie, eds., *Worship and the Hebrew Bible: Essays in Honour of John T. Willis,* JSOTSup 284 (Sheffield: Sheffield Academic Press, 1999) 142–47.

object and source of beauty that beckons one to participate in that beauty by embracing its instruction.

It would be mistaken to relate the two sections of the psalm believing that the first section admits the availability of knowledge of God through creation and the second makes that knowledge more explicit through Torah. As Walter Harrelson suggests, "Esthetic and moral considerations are closely woven together in both parts of the psalm."[16] And the psalmist admits freely the possibility of "misreading" Torah (and likely creation as well) in the petition of verses 12-13. For the one who hears and follows the voice of God in either creation or Torah, God is ultimately the one who can clear or make one innocent.

As a "stand alone" psalm, Psalm 19 has little to say about monarchy. But when read in conjunction with Psalm 18 (and, as we'll see, Pss 20 and 21) it has a function not unlike Psalm 1. Kingship and Torah are linked. The precise nature of that relationship is always up for negotiation. But the connection exists and offers a strong proposal for monarchy.

Psalms 20 and 21 may be considered together quickly. Both are typically designated Royal Psalms because of their focus upon the king.[17] The mention of God's "anointed" in Psalm 20:7 recalls mention of God's anointed in 18:50 (cf. 2:2) and links it to the references to king in Psalm 21. Notice also that it is from the celestial temple that God heard and responded in Psalm 18, and the petition for help in Psalm 20:6 requests that God answer from heaven. Psalm 20 is a prayer for God to help the king and Psalm 21 is a thanksgiving for the help that God rendered. The two psalms together are quite comparable to the movement in Psalm 18.

McCann is correct in observing that Psalms 20 and 21 focus upon God who is first petitioned and who next responds favorably to the request.[18] When the grouping of Psalms 18–21 is considered together, one can observe that the well-being of the king depends upon YHWH. But this is the king who knows about the beauty and expectations of Torah and the king who prays. This is, as Psalms 18 and 20 affirm, YHWH's anointed child/king. God is front and center, the texts are theological—but they are more.

[16] Harrelson, "Psalm 19," 142.

[17] For example, J. Clinton McCann, "The Book of Psalms," *New Interpreter's Bible* (Nashville: Abingdon, 1996) 757. Craigie calls Psalms 20 and 21 a royal liturgy (*Psalms 1–50*, 184–93).

[18] McCann, "The Book of Psalms," 757.

If we were reading the psalms in relative isolation, we could stop here. However, this is a story of the established monarchy. This is an episode in a developing plot, and theology is never done in a vacuum. The texts under consideration are also political. Maybe God should be (and in fact, actuality is) front and center, but kings can be reluctant to share the spotlight. In the narrative of Israel's story, the fusion of YHWH, Torah, and kingship in Psalms 18–21 is no more innocent than the ark's transferal to Jerusalem under David, or the geographical proximity of Solomon's Temple to his palace. Religion is a powerful and seductive means of legitimating social agendas.[19] Consequently, readers of these texts must be prepared to hear the bold proposal of monarchy—supported by YHWH and Torah—that is offered here.

The next voice of proposal that I will call upon is *Psalm 45*. The psalm is generally described as a Royal Psalm,[20] but beyond this it is remarkably distinct from any other piece in the Psalter. The noun "king" is repeated more times in Psalm 45 (seven times in the Hebrew) than in any other psalm, thus underscoring the subject matter of the text. Distinct also is the introductory verse that identifies the purpose of the song. Like an intrusive narrator,[21] the poet steps from behind the scenes as one who "speaks my work to the king" (NRSV—"address my verses to the king," v. 1). Accordingly, the words of the psalm are addressed to the king (vv. 2-9), the queen to be (vv. 10-13a), to an unidentified third party (vv. 13b-15), and finally to the king once more (vv. 16-17).[22] This is no prayer to God. In fact, the only clear references to God appear in verses 2 and 7. Rather, this is the work of a scribe who has composed a wedding song to be used at the marriage of a king and queen. As such, the psalm is remarkable for its secular tone.

---

[19] For example, Peter Berger writes, "religious legitimation purports to relate the humanly defined reality to ultimate, universal and sacred reality. The inherently precarious and transitory constructions of human activity are thus given the semblance of ultimate security and permanence" (Berger, *The Sacred Canopy* [Garden City, N.J.: Doubleday, 1967] 35–36).

[20] For example, Kraus, *Psalms 1–59*, 453; Craigie, *Psalms 1–50*, 337.

[21] On narration, see Mark Allan Powell, *What Is Narrative Criticism?* Guides to Biblical Scholarship (Minneapolis: Fortress, 1990) 26.

[22] There are a number of difficulties with the Hebrew text of this psalm that make a clear structural division difficult and tentative. See Kraus, *Psalms 1–50*, 451–53.

The poem is steeped in flattery for the king. One might even think of it as a poetic exposition of 1 Samuel 16:18, where David first comes to the attention of Saul. In search for a musician to calm his fits of madness, one of Saul's servants says, "Behold, I have seen a son of Jesse the Bethlehemite who knows how to play—a man of valor, a man of war and of understanding speech, a man of form; and YHWH is with him." In Psalm 45, the king is the fairest of all men, and the possessor of God's grace and blessing (v. 2). The king's prowess in battle and his enduring throne are touted, along with the opulence of his palace with ivory and music (vv. 3-9). Amazingly, the king is even addressed as ʾĕlōhîm: God![23] There are no words of royal critique to be found. This is a bold proposal for the beauty of kingship. We can well imagine that just as the queen to be was called "to bow to him [i.e., the king—v. 11]," nonroyal subjects were called to bow all the lower.

While royal ideology is clear, the psalm does sound its theological notes. The king is blessed by God (v. 2). At least part of the king's responsibility calls for the king to stand for truth (v. 4). And of course the king is called God's anointed (mšḥ, v. 7). As McCann writes, "while the king could be lavishly honored and addressed, and while the events of his life could be opulently celebrated, it is clear that his power is finally derivative."[24] These are important points to register, and all the more so because they square with the theological underpinnings found in other monarchic proposals in the Psalms. Perhaps in the task of preaching and teaching in congregations, this is where the emphasis should be placed. Still, failure to see the ideology of kingship that is religiously legitimated is tantamount to turning Qoheleth into an optimist.

Psalm 72, in its canonical form, is a transitional poem. On the one hand it brings the era of David to a close: "Ended are the prayers of David, son of Jesse" (v. 20). To be sure, this verse originally may have concluded

---

[23] This is the exact translation of the Hebrew, although the difficulty of this meaning has led scholars to look for likely emendations to the text. For example, see Craigie, *Psalms 1–50*, 336–37. Notions of deified kings were not unheard of in the ancient Near East, especially in Egypt. On the whole, Israel rejected such outright claims. However, the high ideology of kingship in the ancient world sometimes seems to have been seductive in elaborate descriptions of the king. Perhaps the closest counterpart to Psalm 45:6 is the language in Isaiah 9:6 where a Davidic heir is called "mighty God."

[24] McCann, "The Book of Psalms," 863.

a Davidic collection comprised of Psalms 51 and following, and not specifically Book Two.[25] And it is also the case that other Davidic Psalms follow Psalm 72, especially in Book 5 (Pss 107–50). But coming after so many psalms that have centered on David, and given that only three Davidic psalms occur in Books Three and Four (Pss 86, 101, 103), Psalm 72 does sound a note of closure. This is all the more so when the superscription, "Of Solomon," is taken into consideration. Solomon is the successor, the son who will attempt to carry forward the throne of his father. David's era has come to end but the monarchy moves forward. The precise nature of that monarchy is the subject matter of Psalm 72.

Verses 1-7 are framed by references to righteousness *(ṣdq)*. Verses 1-2 are crucial for the meaning of the Psalm. They may be translated, rather literally, like this:

> God, your *justice* to the *king* give, and your righteousness to a *son of the king*.
> May he judge *your people* in righteousness, and *your oppressed* in *justice*.

As McCann has observed, the chiastic structure of this verse surrounds the king and God's people with justice.[26] First, it is important to note that kingship is to be imbued with divine righteousness and justice. Just as the legitimacy to rule as king in Psalm 2 was derivative (from God), here the characteristics of the king's rule are derivative. Second, kingship is to be for the well-being of the people of God—a rationale that accords well with 1 Samuel 9:16 where kingship also is envisioned to benefit God's people. The connection between 1 Samuel 9:16 and Psalm 72:4 is further strengthened because both texts maintain that the king specifically is to be about the business of "saving" *(yšʿ)* people.[27]

The psalmist turns to the arena of creation in an effort to elaborate more fully the character of the king's rule. There is a beneficent orderliness to the king's reign that is as dependable as day and night, and as sustaining as the rain is for people whose existence is intimately linked to agricultural success. The well-being *(šālôm)* that results from the king's rule will endure as long as the moon itself (vv. 5-7).

---

[25] For example, McCann, "The Book of Psalms," 964.

[26] On this point see McCann and the sources that he references, "The Book of Psalms," 963.

[27] See Chapter Two above.

Verses 8-14 envision the near universal rule of the king, and offer a reason why he should have such far-reaching authority. The language in verse 8 about ruling "from sea to sea and from the river to the ends of the earth" should not be pressed into the mold of cartography. For one thing, the poet is making use of the literary device of merismus: the expression of a totality by means of contrasting parts. The meaning of the verse is roughly equivalent to saying "from East to West, and North to South, and everything in between." For another thing, the language of "sea" (*yam*) and "river" (*nāhar*) are evocative of mythological motifs in the ancient Near East, and Ras Shamra in particular. In the Ugaritic texts discovered there, the Canaanite deity Baʿal does battle against the chaotic waters of Yam and Nahar as an act of establishing order in the world. To find those terms in Psalm 72, which talks about the realm of creation in one breath and enemies submitting to Israel's king in the next, may well connote that the king's dominion extends over natural and historical threats. Also noteworthy, this language of universal dominion and of kings and nations serving Israel's king is a point of contact with the elevated language about the king that we saw in Psalm 2.

In the view of Psalm 72, this expansive reign is justified because of the king's compassion for the weak. Verse 12 is introduced by the particle *kî* that is frequently to be understood causally, i.e., "because." The text from the end of verse 11 through the beginning of verse 12 can be read, "All the nations—may they serve him [i.e., the king], *because* he delivers the needy when they cry." The king's entitlement to reign is based upon his compassion for those in need. As in verse 4, in verse 13 the king embodies the positive view of monarchy in 1 Samuel 9:16 when the psalmist exclaims: "And the lives of the needy, *he saves.*"

Verses 15-17 are essentially a petition for the well-being of the good king whose rule both saves the needy (vv. 12-14) and results in the abundance of produce in the realm of nature (v. 16). The generous set of circumstances envisioned by the psalm is not for Israel alone, but—in language evocative of Genesis 12—extends to the nations who themselves are blessed by the king's reign.[28]

Verses 18-19 seem to be a benediction intended to conclude Book Two and thus not originally a part of Psalm 72. However, if they are taken

[28] For some remarks on the connection between Psalm 72:17 and Genesis 12:1-3, see McCann, "The Book of Psalms," 964.

together with the thought of the psalm they remind Israel that God is the one who makes possible the beneficial rule of the king and thus is the one who deserves praise. And, as discussed above, verse 20 appears to be a marker that once concluded a collection of Davidic psalms. As suggested earlier, the force of the verse here adds a transitional character to Psalm 72.

Psalm 72 is cast as a prayer to God, and so makes theological claims about the rule of God. It is God's justice and righteousness, mediated by the king, that results in the well-being of the social and natural worlds. This is one of those remarkable texts that refuses to compartmentalize the world by speaking of humans or creation in isolation from one another. The psalm affirms that God's justice and righteousness are holistic in scope and encompass the entire world order.

The psalm is also personal. On the one hand, it expresses the longings of one who has seen the struggles of the weak and needy and who desires that their causes be championed. On the other hand, the prayer lacks the pathos of those who themselves cry out in need. It sounds more like the prayer of one who has some vested interest in the continuation of monarchy. Whether that interest is wealth, power, or both cannot be known, but it does seem certain that the one offering the petition is not asking for great change.[29]

The socio-political aspects of Psalm 72 are easy to spot. It is a bold plea for the perpetuation of monarchy, but not just any kind of monarchy. The psalm holds out high promise for the society ruled by the right kind of king. To be sure, there is a certain irony that such a positive psalm has a Solomonic title because Solomon's leadership frequently was far from compassionate. In fact, 1 Kings 12 places the blame for the division of the united monarchy squarely on the harsh policies of Solomon.[30] But there is none of that in Psalm 72. At the conclusion of Books One and Two, the psalm underscores the defining character of YHWH's anointed

---

[29] I make this statement realizing that if the psalm is isolated from Israel's story in the Book of Psalms (emergence, establishment, collapse, and reemergence) it may be heard quite differently. For people in post-monarchic Israel, the psalm may have been heard messianically. In this context, the psalm could be heard as a yearning for radical social change that calls for the demise of foreign rule and the implementation of Israelite kingship under the guidance of a merciful leader. This is a splendid example of the dynamic relationship that exists among canon, culture, and context.

[30] I will return to this amazing irony a bit later.

who has been placed on Zion's holy mountain by God (Ps 2:6). Monarchy, rightly construed, is the form of social organization through which the justice and righteousness of God are conveyed to the world and for the world.

The gist of the discussion so far has been to suggest that the Royal Psalms, supported by Torah claims, present a bold proposal of monarchy in the first two books of the Psalter. It is typical of these psalms to exhibit personal, social, and theological interests. The psalms do not deny that YHWH reigns, but neither are they socially and personally disinterested. Ecclesiastical readings may prefer to focus upon the theological, and perhaps personal, dimensions of these texts and that is important. Such a focus stands as a reminder that any form of social organization is ultimately answerable to a God who desires the well-being of all creation. But ecclesiastical readings also should remember the powerful political proposal that is embedded in the claim to be God's anointed king. People in the pews who live in democratic societies may forget the temptations and dangers that exist when power and means are concentrated in the hands of a few.[31] The recent collapse of major corporations in the United States that has directly and indirectly impacted thousands upon thousands of people might stand as a graphic reminder of such dangers. It should come as no surprise, then, that the first two books of the Psalter contain not only the bold proposal for monarchy. The pained voice of protest also comes through loud and clear.

Voices of Protest

Despite kingly claims to the contrary, all was not well under David—or any other king for that matter. I will now consider three levels of protest against the bold claims of monarchy by moving from the subtle to the explicit.

As noted earlier, Psalm 72 is a transitional voice. It brings to an end "the prayers of David son of Jesse" and passes the established monarchy on to Solomon. By virtue of God's grant of righteousness and justice, the world and its creatures prosper under the rule of the new king. But the informed reader will remember Solomon's twelve tax districts (1 Kgs 4), the forced labor demanded of Israelites themselves (1 Kgs 5:13), the amass-

---

[31] This not to suggest that democratic societies are immune to corruption, for such is surely not the case!

ing of horses, chariots, and wealth (1 Kings 10:26-29). The wise reader will remember the words of Solomon's son, Rehoboam: "My father made heavy your yoke, but I, I will add to your yoke" (1 Kgs 12:14). To be sure, this is not the only side to Solomon's character; but it is a very persistent trait. The reader of Psalm 72, with its Solomonic superscription, is at some odds to explain the disparity between the claims of the psalm and the actual rule of Solomon.[32] It is an ironic combination and, I would suggest, a subtle challenge to the high claims of monarchy that permeate the body of the psalm. Anyone tracing Israel's story in the Book of Psalms would have to pause at Psalm 72 and wonder about the future of monarchy before moving to Book Three.

If the subtle suggestion of the title of Psalm 72 is a crack in the wall of the monarchic proposal, it is preceded by less subtle markers. Of the twelve superscriptions in Books One and Two that associate a psalm with an event from David's life (as narrated in the Books of Samuel) no less than nine of them show David either running or hiding for his life.[33] Most of these make reference to David in flight from Saul. However, the most telling superscription may be the one of Psalm 3 that portrays David in flight from his son Absalom. This desperate flight follows right on the heels of the sterling introduction of God's anointed in Psalm 2. The point, then, is this: Despite the voices of support for monarchy, there are less than subtle clues that the establishment of kingship had some built-in difficulties from the beginning.

Clearly the loudest voices of protest in the Book of Psalms are the laments, or prayers. There are, in fact, far more of these than any other single type of psalm in the Psalter. In contrast to the view offered by Psalm 72, where the king reigns justly, where the poor and needy are cared for and there is an abundance of produce, the Book of Psalms is numerically weighted toward those who are pressed hard by injustice, hatred, and want. The cause of truth defended by the king, of which Psalm 45:4 boasts,

---

[32] See Clinton McCann's very perceptive and helpful comments on this disparity in "The Book of Psalms," 964–65. Among other things, he writes: "The disparity between Psalm 72 and the actual monarchy represents the disparity that always exists between the will of God and every attempt to implement the will of God concretely in space and time. The same disparity is evident, for instance, when we call the church 'the body of Christ' and then observe the actual behavior of the church" (Ibid., 965).

[33] These are: Psalms 3, 18, 34, 52, 54, 56, 57, 59, 63. The remaining psalms are 7, 51, 60.

is called into question by the outcry of the laments. In fact, no fewer than half of the first seventy-two psalms in the Psalter are laments.[34] No other "party" can muster that many votes. The claims of the ruler on behalf of the kingdom are not lived realities.

At least thirty-two of the laments in Books One and Two are attributed to David, in one way or another, by their titles. There are eighteen laments that mention David in conjunction with the vocabulary of prayer or liturgical instructions (Pss 4, 5, 6, 9/10, 12, 13, 17, 22, 31, 38, 39, 41, 55, 58, 61, 64, 69, 70). Another ten psalms begin with historical references (Pss 3, 7, 51, 52, 54, 56, 57, 59, 60, 63). Finally, there are four laments that begin only with *lĕdāvid* ("to/of/by/for/belonging to David"). These are Psalms 25, 26, 28, and 35.

Although almost any lament could provide a port of entry to consider protests against the royal agenda, it is this last grouping that interests me. In addition to the laments there are only two other psalms in the first two books of the Psalter that begin simply with *lĕdāvid*: Psalms 27 and 37. As we will see, each of these two psalms registers its own protest against the notion of "David reigns."

It is widely acknowledged that the preposition, *l*, of *lĕdāvid*, has a number of possible meanings.[35] Without adequate context it is difficult to determine the syntactic function of the prefix, and the brief titles of the psalms offer precious little context. Consequently, different generations of readers have held different opinions. Most critical scholars would be inclined to understand the expression to mean "dedicated to David," or "belonging to the Davidic collection." This or some similar interpretation may be exactly correct, but I would like to suggest that we shift the point of view a bit. Imagine the psalm not being heard as a voice dedicated to David, however that might be construed. Could the psalm, so headed, be heard as a voice addressed simply "to" David? To be sure, the psalms that bear these titles are in the first instance prayers to God. But are not prayers sometimes overheard? Are they not sometimes *intended* to be overheard? Could these psalms function rather like "letters to the edi-

---

[34] Counts of this sort are always subject to dispute. For example, Psalm 27 contains elements of confidence and lament. Determining the genre will depend upon where the interpreter places the accent. This not withstanding, it is widely agreed that laments are the dominant single category in the Psalter.

[35] See, for example, the comments by Craigie, *Psalms 1–50*, 33–34.

tor" or "calls to the talk show host" to say *to David* that all is not well in the kingdom? Could such psalms invite not only God to listen but also God's anointed to listen and respond to the plights of the people? It is certainly an interpretive possibility worthy of consideration.

Psalm 25 is an acrostic poem where each line begins with successive letters of the Hebrew alphabet. This form helps draw together a number of topics that otherwise are not clearly related. Or to put it another way, the orderly structure of the psalm provides a sense of order to one who feels threatened on many fronts: enemies (vv. 2, 19); the need for divine instruction (vv. 4-5, 8, 12); sin and guilt (vv. 7, 11, 18); loneliness, affliction, and distress (vv. 16b-17); perhaps even forsaken by God, since the poet asks God to "turn and be gracious" (v. 16a). The prayer is bracketed by the psalmist's assertion of trust in God (v. 2) and a resolve to wait for God's response (v. 21). Importantly, the final petition ("Redeem, O God, Israel from all of its troubles."—v. 22) suggests that the disequilibrium experienced by the poet is not only personal but extends to the whole of Israel. Also, the verb used for "redeem" *(pdh)* does not necessarily carry moral connotations. That is, redemption is not merely a spiritual transaction. For example, this is the same word used when the people "redeem" or "ransom" Jonathan from Saul. There, a rash vow by the king placed the Israelite troops in jeopardy by not allowing them to eat. Unaware of the vow, Jonathan ate some honey. Upon discovering the deed, Saul was bent on killing his son until the troops rose up and redeemed Jonathan. In an ironic twist, instead of being a redeemer the king was on the verge of infanticide (1 Sam 14:24-46). In Psalm 25 the psalmist wisely asks for *God* to redeem Israel.

The psalm is theological throughout as it calls upon God for help and recounts divine attributes (i.e., God is merciful, steadfast, good, and upright—v. 6-8). For the psalmist there is only one source of protection, forgiveness, and comfort: God. Not only does this hold true for the poet but for the larger society as well.

Psalm 26 is a prayer that asks for YHWH's judgment—in fact, demands it. In language that is typical of Israel's prayers, the psalmist commands YHWH to judge her or him (v. 1). The language of demand continues in verse 2 with the command that YHWH examine and test the interior being of the psalmist. The opening verses affirm the poet's integrity, trust, and faithfulness (v. 1-3). Confidence reigns and there is no fear of God's judgment. The rest of the psalm develops these themes. Verses 4 and 5 are evocative of Psalm 1 where clear distinctions between the wicked and the righteous are drawn. Here the psalmist disavows the company of the wicked—a further qualification for YHWH's positive judgment. Verses 6-8 may reflect some liturgical act connected with the Temple, and some have even called this an entrance liturgy (along with Pss 15 and 24).[36] However, liturgy lies buried beneath literature and in the context of Israel's story the references to approaching God's altar and house are further affirmations of the psalmist's innocence. Similar to Psalm 25, this text ends with a plea for redemption (*pdh*—v. 11) and a corporate reference, here to the worshiping assembly (*mqhlym*—v. 12)—as opposed to the assembly of the wicked (v. 6).

The precise reason for this prayer is uncertain. But for our purposes it is sufficient to note that circumstances are sufficiently bad that the psalmist must turn to YHWH for vindication and redemption. In this connection it is important to remember that one of the reasons the people offered to Samuel in their request for a king concerned this whole issue of judgment. There the people wanted a king to rule or "judge" *(špt)* them (1 Sam 8:20). In the view of Psalm 26:1, however, something seems amiss. The psalmist must turn to YHWH for judgment *(špt)!* And like Psalm 25, the psalmist of Psalm 26:11 calls to YHWH (and not the Davidic king) for redemption.

Theologically, God vindicates and redeems. Personally, the poet is vindicated. Socially, the accusers will be shown to be wrong and the psalmist will rightfully stand with the community in worship. Between the plea for vindication (v. 1) and redemption (v. 11) the poet awaits in trust and confidence. The prayer has been offered and the psalmist looks to a new future.

Psalm 27 is striking in the way that it blends affirmation in YHWH and admission of trouble. The psalm may be divided broadly into two sections: verses 1-6 and 7-14. While it is tempting to say that the first section expresses affirmation and the second section admits trouble, the poem is more complex than this.

The first section of the psalm (vv. 1-6) is framed by references to YHWH: two in verse 1 and one in verse 6. At the center of the unit (v. 4) stand three

---

[36] See McCann's discussion of these suggestions, "The Book of Psalms," 781–82. If one should press the issue of historical setting, it is more likely that Kraus is correct in seeing the prayer as offered by one who has fled to the Temple seeking asylum after being accused falsely (*Pss 1–59*, 325–26).

references to YHWH that come in staccato fashion: "asked from YHWH;" "house of YHWH;" "beauty of YHWH." Verses 2-3 and 5-6a admit the existence of adversaries and enemies. The structure of the unit surrounds the enemies by the divine presence. Also, the references to adversaries are made with an air of confidence and not fearfulness. Still, the all-encompassing presence of YHWH does not preclude the existence of enmity.

The second unit is dominated by the tone of petition.[37] This unit too is framed by references to YHWH. In verse 7 prayer is addressed to YHWH, and in verses 13-14 YHWH is the source confidence. Each major petition that occurs between the framing verses contains a direct appeal to YHWH. The overriding concern of the poet seems to be an assurance of God's presence (vv. 8-10) and deliverance from "deceitful witnesses" (vv. 11-12). If it is true that in the first section YHWH's presence does not prevent enmity, then it may be claimed that in the second section enmity does not preclude the presence of YHWH.

Taken as a whole the psalm, like its units, is framed by references to YHWH. The two references to YHWH in verse 1, paired with the three references in verse 14, surround the inescapable struggle with adversity with the divine presence. Together, the beginning and end of the psalm exude confidence and patience—a stance that befits the community of believers.

As one of the voices that narrates Israel's story in the Psalter, this psalm is relentlessly Yahwistic. Sheer repetition of the divine name alone makes this point. But more significant is the affirmation that YHWH is "my salvation" (yš‘) in verse 1 and the designation of YHWH as the "God of my salvation" (yš‘) in verse 9. Although the Davidic king is charged with the task of saving God's people, this poet is clear that only YHWH is capable of providing deliverance from the troubles at hand. So we can sense the personal anguish of the poet in the psalm's verses. We can see also that this singer has her or his theology in place and has an abiding hope in God. But we see too that the text has its socio-political edge in its admission of enemies and affirmation that YHWH (read, "not the Davidic king") is the source of salvation.

Psalm 28 is the fourth "to David" psalm in succession. As with many psalms, there is room to debate the genre of this song. Depending upon

---

[37] Kraus calls the section a "prayer song of a person persecuted and accused" (*Psalms 1–59*, 332).

where in the psalm one places the accent, it might be labeled a lament
(vv. 1-5) or a thanksgiving (vv. 6-9). Some have even considered Psalm 28
to be a Royal Psalm.[38] Given that most laments make a turn toward
affirmation or thanksgiving, the designation of lament—or perhaps even
prayer song, as Kraus suggests[39]—seems appropriate.

The opening verses (1-2) concern voice. The psalmist pleads to be
heard by YHWH and yearns for a divine response. If this prayerful transaction of speech and listening should fail to occur, the poet's future is surely
death (*bôr*—the Pit or Sheol). Life hangs on the power of healing conversation with YHWH.

In verses 3-5 the poet petitions God to be spared the fate of the
wicked. In particular, the psalmist is threatened by those who speak kindly
(*šālôm*) but have evil intent (*rʿh*) in their hearts. These are the people who
do not discern the hand of YHWH in the world around them and therefore deserve to suffer the consequences brought on by their own hands.

Verses 6-7 take an amazing turn toward rejoicing and praise. Some
have argued that between verses 5 and 6 lies a liturgical act, perhaps a
priestly oracle of salvation that accounts for the shift of mood.[40] The literature simply obscures the liturgical act. By way of analogy one might think
of 1 Samuel 1 where Eli, upon correctly understanding Hannah's prayer at
the Shiloh temple, announces: "Go in peace." This may well be what has
happened in Psalm 28, but such an explanation is by no means necessary.
That is, there is something about the mystery of conversation—of speaking
and being heard, genuinely heard by one who cares—that engenders new
life and previously unseen possibilities. Such is the nature of prayer.

Verses 8 and 9 round out the psalm with an affirmation and final petition. Verse 8 might seem to pose a challenge to the line of interpretation that I have followed to this point. The verse may be translated:

YHWH is the strength of his people,[41]
   and a refuge, salvation of his anointed is he.

---

[38] On the possible genres, see McCann, "The Book of Psalms," 789.

[39] Kraus, *Psalms 1–59*, 339.

[40] See ibid., 341.

[41] There seems to be a problem with the MT here and most translators follow a host
of ancient witnesses and read "his people."

The question is: How can a psalm that speaks favorably of YHWH's anointed be any sort of protest against the institution of monarchy? The typical assumption that the expression "his anointed" in this verse points directly to the king may be correct, but it is not without room for challenge. In the parallelism of the verse the phrases "his people" and "his anointed" are synonymously paired. How are we to take this? When the term "anointed" occurs elsewhere in the Psalter the context, and more often than not the parallelism, clearly links it with the king and/or with David (e.g., Pss 18:50; 132:10, 17). This occurs even outside of the Psalter, as in 2 Chronicles 6:42. The closest parallel to Psalm 28:8 is Habakkuk 3:13 where "your people" and "your anointed" stand as parallel terms. In neither text is there sufficient context to specify exactly who is intended by the designation anointed. Now we know from Isaiah 45:1 that the term can be applied to a non-Israelite king because Cyrus of Persia is called God's "anointed." Even more suggestive is the historical Psalm 105, where God's "anointed ones" unmistakably refers to "my prophets" (v. 15; this verse has a parallel in 1 Chron 16:22). Could Psalm 28:8 be urging a radical democratization of the concept of the anointed one by suggesting that all of God's people are anointed? The care that God is petitioned to offer to all of God's people in verse 9 would certainly support this possibility.

Even if the term anointed in 28:8 refers to the king, the verse still has a democratizing effect as it places the king and the people equally dependent upon YHWH. James Mays writes, "the psalm holds the individual, the anointed, and the people of the LORD together in that inseparable unity which belongs to the purpose of God."[42] And notice, once again, that it is YHWH and not the king who is asked "to save" the people, as well as "shepherd" them. Kings and rulers in the ancient Near East were frequently referred to as shepherds (cf. Ezekiel 34). For the psalmist, the only suitable shepherd is YHWH.

Psalm 28 may seem less bold in its protest than others, but in its admission that trouble has not been put down, in its democratizing tendencies, and in its turn to YHWH and not king for salvation and shepherding, it surely lodges its own voice of protest.

Psalm 35 is a long and somewhat complicated text. It seems best described as a lament or prayer song,[43] although other designations have

[42] Mays, *Psalms*, 135.

[43] For example, McCann, "The Book of Psalms," 818; Kraus, *Psalms 1–59*, 392.

been given.[44] The psalm seems most naturally divided into three sections, each of which concludes on a note of praise: 1-10, 11-18, 19-28. Legal, military, and hunting images are found in the first section. The threats of harmful witnesses and sickness are present in the second section. And the third section takes up treacherous words and taunting by enemies. A clear explanation for the movement from one section to the next is not readily available. McCann may be right when he suggests that we interpret "the apparent literary disarray as an appropriate indication of the chaotic conditions that prevailed in the life of the psalmist."[45]

While there are many ways to approach the psalm, one that interests me is that each section is much concerned about speech and each section features a reversal in the kind of speech that is offered. The psalm opens with the imperative verb, "contend" *(rîbāh)*. It is a legal term and is tantamount to saying "Lay out your case." The psalmist insists that YHWH place on trial those who would try him or her. Legal and military images blur and signal the seriousness of the situation that leads the poet to give voice to the words so desired from YHWH: "Your salvation am I" (v. 3). Verses 4-8 ask God to repay the adversaries in the same currency that they are attempting to deal out to the psalmist. Verse 5a, "Let them be like chaff before the wind," is evocative of Psalm 1 where the wicked are described as chaff driven by the wind. This allusion clearly places the adversaries in Psalm 35 among the wicked. Just as the section began with speech, verses 9-10 conclude it with speech. The life-saving salvation desired in verse 3 gives way to a life *(nepeš)* that rejoices in God's salvation. Even the psalmist's bones ponder the incomparability of YHWH who sides with the weak and the needy.[46]

The second section (vv. 11-18) also begins and ends with speech. The mention of harmful or violent *(ḥms)* witnesses in verse 11 has legal connotations and recalls verse 1. In a culture that did not have DNA analysis, fingerprinting, or security cameras life itself could hang on the veracity of one's speech and certainly one's character could be much affected by

---

[44] Craigie, for example, believes the psalm is a Royal Psalm *(Psalms 1–50*, 285). The military images in the first part of Psalm 35 leads him to this conclusion. However, Craigie attaches more freight to the words than the metaphorical language can bear and his interpretation appears forced.

[45] McCann, "The Book of Psalms," 818.

[46] Cf. Mays, *Psalms*, 155.

words. Whereas the psalmist had offered prayers for his accusers when they faced trouble, they return "evil instead of good" (v. 12). The poet turns to YHWH for rescue and promises to offer thanksgiving and praise in the congregation.

The final section (vv. 19-28) opens with the rejoicing of the psalmist's enemies and with their treacherous words. "Their mouths are opened wide against me" says the poet and filled with taunts (v. 21). To make matters worse, the one who should speak—i.e., YHWH—remains silent! The psalmist pleads for God to intervene and to offer judgment/vindication (*špṭ*—v. 24). In anticipation of divine judgment, the poet can now sing "My tongue will declare your righteousness. . . ."

The entire psalm turns on the reversal of speech as the language shifts from contention, harmful testimony, and treacherous words to rejoicing, thanksgiving, and praise. This transformation is enabled by conversation with God who saves (*yšʿ*—vv. 3, 9) and judges or vindicates (*špṭ*—v. 24). As we have seen before, these are the activities that are the responsibility of the ruling king. From the psalmist's point of view, all is not well in the kingdom and the only recourse is YHWH, who pays attention to the weak and the needy.

Psalm 37 is typically labeled a wisdom psalm. There are many reasons for this designation. It is an acrostic, and every other line begins with a successive letter of the Hebrew alphabet. The contrast between the righteous and the wicked, so characteristic of the wisdom literature, is a prominent aspect of Psalm 37. Terms for the wicked occur fifteen times and those for the righteous occur nine times. Verse 16 is a proverb, and the didactic character of the psalm is evident throughout. Finally, it deals with the perplexing problem of the presence of evil in God's good world. The issue of theodicy (narrowly understood as "the justice of God") is frequently a subject of wisdom material.

The acrostic form that orders the psalm makes it essentially impossible to find smaller units. The whole must be taken together. But, verses 1-4 basically outline the thought of the poem. Believers should understand that the prosperity of the wicked is temporary, and that they should "Trust in YHWH and do good" (v. 3). As such, there is an eschatological edge to the psalm. But as McCann rightly acknowledges, "to live eschatologically means not only to live *for* the future but also to live *by* the future. Living by faith and hope has a profound impact on the present, in terms of emotion and behavior."[47] The didactic tone of the psalm urges present action that is guided by future hope.

It may seem odd to consider a wisdom psalm to be a voice of protest against the establishment, especially since the scribal groups associated with wisdom are frequently believed to have been connected to the royal establishment. But, knowingly or unknowingly, this voice does lodge its protest. First, the very admission that the righteous ones suffer and the wicked fare well is an assault on the monarchic claim that all is well. Unexplained suffering is a reality that challenges the status quo. Next, while the psalm is much concerned about the prosperity of the wicked, it is intensely interested in YHWH. The divine name appears 15 times in the text.[48] The voice of Psalm 37 does not look to the king for help. Instead, as verses 39-40 affirm, salvation (*yšʿ*) and help (*ʿzr*) are to be found in YHWH.

In their admission of trouble, conflict, and adversity, and in their appeal to YHWH for a hearing for redemption, salvation, and shepherding these six *lĕdāvid* ("to David") psalms acknowledge that all is not well in the kingdom. At an address to the Davidic monarch, each voice urges the king to take a look at what's really going on. People are sick, the righteous ones are wrongly accused, and the wicked are prospering. Again and again the people must look to God for help because the governmental "safety net" has come unraveled. What is more, the voices in these psalms are not unique in their outcry. There are many witnesses in Books One and Two to testify that monarchy is not living up to its soteriological and communal responsibilities.

Preliminary Observations

In the intense discussion of monarchy in Books One and Two of the Psalter, the contrasting voices of proposal and protest can be heard clearly. The voices are interwoven and, indeed, the most frequently heard remarks question the efficacy of monarchy in one way or another. But power is per-

---

[47] McCann, "The Book of Psalms," 828.

[48] The NRSV has obscured this count in its translation. The Hebrew designation for the Deity in verse 13 is *ʾadonai*, which is wrongly translated as the LORD. The upper case letters are supposed to be reserved for the name YHWH. The NIV is correct in translating the word as Lord. In addition, the NRSV (presumably for clarity) inserts LORD in verse 22 when neither *ʾadonai* nor YHWH is to be found.

sistent in its own defense, and the strategic positioning of the promonarchic speakers is decisive. The privilege of power gives monarchy the first say (Pss 1–2), a strong rebuttal to protests (Pss 18–21; 45), and the final summation (Ps 72). In may ways the situation here is the reverse of what we saw in 1 Samuel 8–12 where the antimonarchical voices held the positions of privilege. Those who would protest what the kings propose must speak when, where, and how they can. But speak they do, and their voices are not silenced in this story. There is no adjudication between the competing claims in this episode of establishment. That will await subsequent episodes. But as we overhear this contentious conversation a clue surfaces that might guide our listening.

Canon and Congregation: Listening with God

To view a biblical text as canonical is to acknowledge that believing communities over the years have discerned in that text, in one way or another, the Word of God. Amazingly, I can detect only sixteen psalms where God speaks in the first person, and only six of those occur in the first two books of the Psalter.[49] To be sure, there is considerable narration *about* God in the psalms, but actual speeches *by* God are few and far between.

Now this is not necessarily a new observation. People have long noted that the Book of Psalms is one of the few books in the Bible where people speak to God instead of God speaking to the people. Gone is the booming voice of the Exodus: "I am YHWH your God . . . You shall not have other gods over me" (Exod 20:1, 2). Nowhere to be found is the bold prophetic pronouncement, "Thus says YHWH!" In fact, the psalmists even implore that YHWH "not remain silent" (Ps 35:22)! Details such as these have led some to the mistaken conclusion that the Psalms are not to be used for preaching because they are less the Word of God than the prayers of the people.[50] Further, in many liturgical communities the Psalms repre-

---

[49] This count is based on the punctuation in the NRSV. Biblical Hebrew does not make use of quotation marks and occasionally—especially in poetry—it can be difficult to determine the speaker. The texts are: Psalms 2:6, 7; 12:5; 46:10; 50:5, 7-23; 60:6-8; 68:22-24; 81:6-16; 82:2-4, 6-7; 87:6; 89:3-4, 19-37; 90:3; 95:10-11; 105:11, 15; 108:7-9 (60:6-8); 110:1, 4; 132:11-12, 14-18. Psalm 35:3 contains what the psalmist *hopes* to hear YHWH speak, but falls short as a line spoken directly by God.

[50] James Mays clearly and correctly refutes this misconception in his commentary (*Psalms*, 36–39).

sent a response to the Old Testament lesson instead of a reading themselves and are thus relegated to a kind of secondary status. So what are we to make of this?

No doubt those poets who prayed in their anguish were in search of an answer. But first they were in search of a hearing. "Hear, YHWH, my voice when I call" (27:7), or "Hear the voice of my supplication" (28:2), the psalmists pray. Before any resolution to their troubles could be reached, YHWH must hear. Accordingly, the God we encounter in the Book of Psalms is a God of *restrained speech* and *passionate listening*. In fact, it may not be too much to claim that the faith of the psalmists was predicated upon the conviction that God listens. What might this suggest for congregational life?

To the degree that Israel's period of monarchical establishment resembles Loren Mead's Christendom Paradigm, it would be useful to remember Mead's critique of that period. He writes, "A major difficulty of the Christendom Paradigm was its assumption that there was *one* answer, *one* way. Unfortunately, although the paradigm demanded uniformity, no lasting way was found to achieve it."[51] He also observes that even today congregations may tend to hold on to relics of this Paradigm that "hold us hostage to the past. . . ."[52] I would suggest that if congregations in today's rapidly changing ecology are to infer anything about their own identity and mission from the God portrayed in the Book of Psalms, they must engage in restrained speech and passionate listening.

This suggestion may seem to run counter to the evangelistic task entrusted to the Church to proclaim the Good News of God's redemption. But there are ways to proclaim, and then there are ways to proclaim. We might recall the words of Psalm 19:

> There is no speech and there are no words,
>> not heard is their voice.
> But in all the earth their voice goes out,
>> and to the end of the world, their speech (vv. 3-4b).

---

[51] Loren B. Mead, *The Once and Future Church* (Washington, D.C.: The Alban Institute, 1991) 17.

[52] Ibid., 18.

There is no want of creeds, confessions, and official statements made by the many faith communities that make up the Church. But there may very well be a want of passionate listening.

Each of the frames of reference offered by Nancy Ackermann and the other contributors in *Studying Congregations* implies listening.[53] If one would come to know anything about a congregation's ecology, culture, process, resources, and leadership then that one must listen carefully before rushing to describe. Even the methods that are given for studying congregations can be considered a disciplined form of listening. I suggest that the characterization of God in the Book of Psalms as a passionate listener presents a solid theological rationale for doing congregational study. Social-scientific studies of the Church by disinterested analysts can be immensely valuable in helping congregations to address problems. They have their place. But congregational leaders concerned about the well-being of the people of God are rarely disinterested. For them, questions of why and how to proceed are theological as well as sociological questions and touch the very core of who they are. At this point, the Psalter's portrayal of a God who cares enough to listen attentively to all of the voices of proposal and protest offers guidance.

In his classic volume on pastoral theology, Thomas Oden offers these words of counsel to those who would minister to the sick. I think that they are relevant to every aspect of the Church's ministry:

> Listen empathetically, without defensiveness. Do not hesitate to offer the good news of divine forgiveness at the right time. . . . Do not be afraid of silence. The parishioner may be struggling valiantly for slow-growing self-understanding or difficult language that is not ready at hand. Interruptions may be costly. One may never be able to go back to that previous matchless moment.[54]

What might the Church look like if it adopted the stance of restrained speech and passionate listening? What might the Church look like if it took seriously the biblical affirmation that every human being is created

---

[53] Nancy Ammerman, et al., *Studying Congregations: A New Handbook* (Nashville: Abingdon, 1998).

[54] Thomas C. Oden, *Pastoral Theology: Essentials of Ministry* (San Francisco: Harper & Row, 1983) 257.

in the image of God, as Psalm 8 maintains, and that we have something to learn about God by listening to one another—even babbling infants?

What might the Church look like if denominational institutions spent less money on bulk mailings and more funds on sending people out into congregations and communities armed not with projectors, flip charts, and canned speeches but with listening ears and the single question, "How can we help you live out the Gospel in your community?"

What might sermons sound like if pastors quit recycling the same old homilies and thoughts and began listening anew to the Bible with the aid of fresh resources—but not stopping there? Sermons produced in the study alone are of little worth and, worse, are a betrayal of the witness of Jesus. Again, the words of Thomas Oden are instructive:

> The faithful pastor is willing to go unnoticed in the newspapers while quietly following the poor to their barrios, the sick to their bedsides, the melancholic to their isolation, the alcoholic to their dregs, the sincerely inquiring to their wrenching questions, the grieving to their hope, the dying to their rest. It is only by this outgoing watchfulness that one can "make full proof" of one's ministry (2 Tim 4:5).[55]

Serious listening to the Scriptures and serious listening to the people around us are the stuff of preaching instead of *speaking,* as we so often assume.

What might administration in the Church look like if it were no longer viewed as a form of management and control, but rather as a opportunity to discover new gifts and to empower all parishioners to live out the Gospel in their personal and public lives?

What might religious education, done both by those in denominational and institutional positions and those in the cramped Sunday school rooms in a myriad of congregations, look like if the tenor of interaction was conversation characterized by restrained speech and passionate listening?

On the one hand these queries may sound rather domestic and tame. Some may say, "Nothing new." Perhaps, but I'm not sure that I agree. If taken seriously each of the questions that I've raised means relinquishing power: the power held by denominations, their judicatories, their institutions, and their clergy. If, as I have argued above, Psalm 28 speaks for a democratization of the concept of Israel's "anointed," then the Church's

---

[55] Thomas Oden, *Pastoral Theology,* 170.

mission is no longer only a concern of a specialized and elite group, but it is the ministry of every believer.[56] As the listening God of the Psalms knows, there are plenty of voices on our own doorsteps begging to be heard—for those who have ears to hear.

The challenge, then, for today's congregations is to become listening communities. What better way is there to "proclaim" the God of the Book of Psalms? Kathleen Billman and Daniel Migliore describe the importance of being attentive to the protest and pain cloaked in the voices of lament with these words: "We know of no other way to provide sanctuary for the 'tentative speech' of lament than for church leaders to learn and teach what it means *to listen with understanding and compassion*" (emphasis added).[57] As I suggested in the previous chapter, emerging congregations must continually search for ways to remain listening communities less they become locked into a static cycle that stifles the voices of protest. In this chapter I would claim that even in established churches, where all may seem well on the outside, there exist voices of proposal and protest. Such was the case in the period of Israel's established monarchy. To ignore these voices is, at the least, to risk losing the creative and energizing insights that caring people have to offer. Not all conflict is damaging and some should be embraced creatively rather than suppressed.[58] At the worst, refusal to hear competing voices is to risk tearing the congregation apart. In fact, this is precisely what happened to Israel's monarchy at the death of Solomon—the subject of the next chapter.

Summary

In this chapter I have argued that there are strong voices in Books One and Two of the Psalter that propose monarchy as the legitimate way to save God's people from the threats that would do them in. But there are other voices that protest that all is not well under the king's rule. Although some of these voices are subtle and others are direct, each lodges

---

[56] On the emerging ministry of the laity see, William E. Diehl, *Ministry in Daily Life* (Washington, D.C.: The Alban Institute, 1996).

[57] Kathleen D. Billman and Daniel L. Migliore, *Rachel's Cry: Prayer of Lament and Rebirth of Hope* (Cleveland: United Church Press, 1999) 137–38.

[58] See Carl S. Dudley, "Process: Dynamics of Congregational Life," in *Studying Congregations,* 119.

protest in its own tones. The strong voices of kingship, however, surround and intrude on the voices of protest suggesting that the conversation is not equal and that kings will have their way over subjects. Importantly, Yhwh also plays a major role in this conversation. Although God does seem to hold out some possibilities for monarchy, the Deity is very much in tune to the outcries of protest that all is not well. God refuses to silence these voices of opposition and instead chooses to listen more than speak, knowing that hearing itself can be a healing response.

In turn, I have suggested that in their hasty zeal to proclaim the Gospel, congregations have not always heard the real needs of the people. The portrayal of God in the Psalter as a deity of restrained speech and passionate listening underscores the important role that listening has in the life of believing communities and the study of those communities. Even in congregations where all seems well—perhaps especially in these congregations—there are voices of protest to be heard. To marginalize or to stifle these outcries is to risk the well-being of the community.

To return to the thought of Psalm 19, if the silent beauty and mystery of creation can point to the glory of God, then the passionate listening of the Church can be construed as a form of bold proclamation.

4

Collapse

n the last chapter I advocated for the Church a stance of restrained speech and passionate listening. Theologically, the characterization of God as a listening deity in the psalms commends this stance. Practically, it seems to me that the church historically has been far more fascinated with speaking than listening. The current religious voices coming from AM radios, cable and satellite TVs, Internet web pages—voices that speak but do not listen—are legion and point to the neglected role of listening.

However, passionate listening does not translate into impassivity. Not all silence is commendable. There are some "intentional silences that shield practices" that plead for exposure.[1] For example, nearly two decades ago Marie Fortune graphically highlighted the conspiracy of silence that surrounds sexual violence to the horrible detriment of its victims.[2] Much more recently, the voices that finally have found the courage to tell of the nightmarish experiences of sexual abuse by members of the clergy underscore the insidious side of silence. There is a time for speech.

Perhaps the critical questions are when do we finally speak, and who gets the first say? Who gets the floor first? And while we are scrambling

---

[1] Carl S. Dudley, "Process: Dynamics of Congregational Life," in Nancy Ammerman, et al., *Studying Congregations: A New Handbook* (Nashville: Abingdon, 1998) 121.

[2] Marie Marshall Fortune, *Sexual Violence: The Unmentionable Sin* (Ohio: Pilgrim, 1983).

for the microphone, might there be some people that are too timid, who are too frightened, who are too intimidated to claim their right to voice? Are there those who are "troubled beyond speech," who have been condemned to an exile of silence? And if so, is it any concern of the Church?

According to the fourth chapter of Luke's Gospel, when Jesus returned from the wilderness after his baptism he went home to Nazareth. On Sabbath he was invited to give the "morning homily" at the synagogue and he unrolled the scroll to Isaiah 61 and began to talk about "release," "recovery," and "freedom." At first the congregation wanted to believe, perhaps dared to believe, because this was *their* story: the story of Jubilee. If true, it meant good news for them. But Jesus *shifted the voice* in the story from the insiders to the outsiders. Elijah, he recalled, was sent to a Phoenician woman and his presence with her brought blessing while Israel suffered famine. Elisha went to a foreigner named Naaman and cured his leprosy, while many lepers in Israel went unhealed. Jesus gave priority to, and articulated the voices of, those marginalized by Israel's practiced religion. On the one hand, it was understandable that they didn't like his view of their text. Those in his audience felt themselves victimized by the pervasive and invasive Roman occupation all about them. In their minds the foreigners and all of their misguided ways were the problems. But Jesus took Israel's sacred hope in Scripture and through it allowed the voice of foreigners to be heard! For his efforts, Jesus got tossed from the holy gathering.

When do we finally speak out? Whose voice is invited to sound forth from the podium? Whose voice gets to speak from the chancel, from behind the pulpit, or from behind the Communion table? These are questions with which the church has struggled throughout its history, and certainly questions that pull at us. There may be no simple and enduring answers to such questions because they call for constant renegotiations. But as we listen in on the conversation in Book Three of the Psalter, we may overhear a dialogue that offers suggestions to help us think theologically about voice.

Conversation: Voices at Odds

The voices that advocated and contested monarchy in Psalms 1–72 continue to be heard in Psalms 73–89. However, there is a shift in their tone. The voices of advocacy sound more forced and troubled, while the voices of protest sound more urgent. In many ways the conversation is hauntingly similar to the one revealed by Jeremiah's challenge to those who preach "'Peace, peace!' But there is no peace" (Jer 9:11). There are always those who want to hang onto the illusion that all is well—especially when their positions of power and prestige are at stake. But when the desperate voices finally are heard, mirages vanish like the mists they are and reality casts light upon unholy misconceptions.

Book Three begins on "slippery ground." For one thing, David is all but a memory in Psalms 73–89. His name appears first in the historical Psalm 78 (v. 70). This psalm traces God's benevolence to Israel from the Exodus through the selection of David, and the people's failures to respond faithfully. Although the psalm ends abruptly on a brief positive note, one is left to wonder whether in the long run Israel will respond to kingship any more faithfully than to God's previous actions. Given the powerful community lament that follows immediately in Psalm 79 it is hard to place too much hope on the memory of David in 78:70. Next, David's name appears in the superscription of Psalm 86, but this is a lament that ends with a sense of yearning for help yet to come. Finally, David is remembered in the peculiar Psalm 89 that recalls God's past pledge to David but confronts the present dilemma of a disaster at the hands of the enemy and the demise of the Davidic pledge. In the final analysis, the rhetoric of evoking David's memory will not overcome the reality of collapse that haunts Book Three.

For another thing, *Psalm 73* directly takes up the matter of slipping. The Psalm opens:

> Surely God is good to Israel, to those pure in heart.
> But me—my feet almost slipped (v. 1-2a).

The reason for the poet's wavering is provided as the psalm unfolds. Quite simply, the wicked were prospering very nicely (vv. 4-12) and the psalmist, we are led to assume, was not faring as well despite maintaining a "clean heart" and "innocent hands" (v. 13). In many ways, this is precisely the dilemma posed by hearing Psalm 1 in association with the laments that follow. Sometimes the wicked are not like chaff driven by the wind and the righteous do not flourish like trees by water like the psalmist claims. But the commitment of the poet in Psalm 73 to persevere in spite of appearances, to maintain a clean heart and innocent hands, qualifies her or him access to the sanctuary of God (v. 17; cf. Ps 24). Here, in the sanctuary, the turning point comes for the poet, although the precise reason for the transition remains mysterious. Perhaps, though, that is not as problematic as interpreters sometimes have made it since life-changing moments are often mysterious even to those who experience them.

Verses 18-28 present the conclusion reached by the psalmist as to the fate of the wicked and offer the response the poet will make. First, God has set the wicked on "slippery places" (*bahălāqôt*—v. 18a). Second, the poet resolves "to tell of all your [i.e., God's] works" (v. 28b).

Walter Brueggemann's view of Psalm 73 as the theological center of the Psalter is well taken.[3] It recalls the Torah fidelity advocated by Psalm 1, the struggles of life for those who would cling to Torah—struggles that pervade the book of Psalms—and the joyous telling of the works of God that anticipates the raucous praise at the end of the Psalter. As a voice that speaks at that moment when there is no longer any David, and the transition to David's descendents has given rise to pressing questions, the psalm speaks an assuring word. The mysterious encounter with God in sacred space has been enough to validate the life-style of the psalmist and to reveal the ultimate fate of the wicked. No new actions seem to be called for; the psalmist must simply stay the course and God will set things right at the correct time.

Now the stance advocated by Psalm 73 is not to be taken lightly. Most people within a community of faith can offer their own stories of how beleaguered lives were suddenly snapped back into place during acts of worship. The sacraments and the proclamation of the gospel work their healing in mysterious ways that are to be celebrated. Still, given the place that this psalm's voice is sounded in Israel's story, suspicions rise close to the surface. Peter Berger has described the role of religion in maintaining socially constructed worlds. In particular, religion serves to integrate "into a comprehensive nomos . . . precisely those marginal situations in which the reality of everyday life is put in question."[4] Might not the settlement to the problem of the prosperous wicked arrived at in Psalm 73 represent

[3] Brueggemann, "Bounded by Obedience and Praise," in Patrick D. Miller, ed., *The Psalms and the Life of Faith* (Minneapolis: Fortress, 1995) 189–213; especially 204–13.

[4] Peter Berger, *The Sacred Canopy: Elements of a Sociological Theory of Religion* (Garden City, N.J.: Doubleday, 1967) 42.

a serious effort to maintain a world that is beginning to unravel at the edges? For the moment it is enough to allow the question to linger. There are other voices to be heard.

Psalm 74 urgently presses issues raised by the previous speaker. The prayer has three clearly discernable sections: verses 1-11, 12-17, 18-23.[5] It is clear that there are numerous points of contact between Psalms 73 and 74. Perhaps the most notable ones are that both are troubled by the prosperity of the wicked, and both are also keenly focused upon God's sanctuary (*mqdš*—73:17; 74:7).[6] Yet there are considerable differences.

The individual singer of Psalm 73 arrived at a theodic settlement on the thorny problem of wicked people who prosper: their success was only temporary and they would eventually fall.[7] In the meantime, the poet would be content to be near God (73:28). In Psalm 74 the problem of the wicked has grown exponentially. For one thing, the problem is no longer an individual dilemma but a community matter.[8] The situation lamented by Psalm 73 was far more contagious than that poet had imagined. For another thing, the satisfaction gained from being near God in Psalm 73 gives way in Psalm 74 to the congregation's despair over being cast off and forgotten by God (vv. 1, 2, 19). Finally, while the sanctuary was crucial for the theodic settlement arrived at by the poet of Psalm 73, in Psalm 74 God's sanctuary has been desecrated and destroyed (vv. 3-8). The source of answers for life's unnerving questions has been eliminated.

Scholars have differed over the years about the particular calamity that evoked the voice of Psalm 74. Although the psalm itself offers no irrefutable answer, it is difficult to suppress the image of Jerusalem's fate suffered at the hands of the Babylonians in 587 B.C.E. At the very least,

---

[5] See James L. Mays, *Psalms,* Interpretation (Louisville: Westminster/John Knox, 1994) 244, or J. Clinton McCann, "The Book of Psalms," *New Interpreter's Bible* (Nashville: Abingdon, 1996) 973. Other divisions are possible. For example, see Hans-Joachim Kraus, *Psalms 60–150: A Commentary,* trans. by Hilton C. Oswald (Minneapolis: Fortress, 1989) 96.

[6] For other points of contact between Psalms 73 and 74 see McCann, "The Book of Psalms," 972.

[7] On the expression "theodic settlement," see Walter Brueggemann, *Theology of the Old Testament: Testimony, Dispute, Advocacy* (Minneapolis: Fortress, 1997) 386ff.

[8] Form critics typically regard Psalm 74 as a communal lament or prayer. For example, see Kraus, *Psalms 60–150,* 96; Erhard S. Gerstenberger, *Psalms, Part 2, and Lamentations,* FOTL 15 (Grand Rapids: Eerdmans, 2001) 77; Marvin E. Tate, *Psalms 51–100,* WBC (Waco: Word, 1990) 246.

this voice that speaks early in Book Three foreshadows and anticipates the destruction that will inevitably come.

The ghastly specter of the Temple's destruction is framed by imperatives that direct God to "remember" (vv. 2, 18, 22). In the first instance, the psalmist insists that God remember "your congregation you acquired [or created] of old"(v. 2a).[9] Here the object of God's remembering is Israel. Divine memory can be good for Israel, as in the case of Exodus 2:24 when God's memory was a prelude to deliverance. However, the situation is different in the next two occurrences of the command. Verses 18 and 22 demand that God remember how the enemy "taunts" *(ḥrp)* the Lord. We can reasonably assume that divine memory of enemies is not of the same sort as it is for Israel! Between the insistence on God's benevolent memory for Israel and bitter memory for Israel's enemies lie verses 12-17.

In this hymnic section, Psalm 74:12-17 draws upon ancient cosmogonic images of a deity that overcomes inimical forces to establish the ordered world. The victor of such a battle was typically acknowledged as king. Similar mythic accounts are to be found especially in Mesopotamia and Canaan (Ugarit), and to a lesser extent in Egypt. In Psalm 74, the cosmogonic images of overcoming the sea (*yam*—v. 13) are evocative of God's victory over the sea in Exodus 14–15. Hans-Joachim Kraus is correct in seeing that both creation and salvation images are present in the psalm, and the tendency to choose one over the other is misguided.[10] In fact, creation and exodus images also will be intertwined by the prophetic voice that speaks from the Babylonian exile in Isaiah 40-55. Israel's faith in YHWH as the one who established the ordered world seemed always to become an immense reservoir of inspiration and strength for the people when confronted by overwhelming forces.[11]

The logic of Psalm 74 involves reminding God of the deity's power in establishing the world (vv. 12-17) and to cast Israel's enemies as comparable to the forces that YHWH subdued in primeval moments (vv. 18, 22).

---

[9] The verb *qnh* can covey the sense of "created" (see Kraus, *Psalms 60–150*, 98). Given the mythic and cosmogonic language of verses 12-17 one could make a strong case for translating Psalm 74:2a as "Remember your congregation that you created long ago."

[10] Kraus, *Psalms 60–150*, 99.

[11] The cosmogonic images present in Jewish and Christian apocalyptic literature (e.g., Daniel, Revelation) are also ample testimony of this claim.

It is a plea for God to act in character.[12] For God to remember the congregation that was created long ago (v. 2) calls for the Creator to treat the enemies of Israel no better than the Holy One treated Leviathan. The psalm ends with the insistence that God "not forget your foes" (v. 23).

To recall God's creative power in a situation of upheaval and radical disorientation is no small thing. It is nothing short of an appeal to Israel's canonical memory, to ancient life-giving and sustaining traditions. But the memory of ancient deeds of divine benevolence can produce different effects. First, the memory of God's power in the past can be a daring act of faith that provides courage and guidance for people searching out their bearings in a raging storm of conflict. Biblical faith is frequently characterized exactly by this kind of memory. Second, though, repeating ancient credos can be a desperate act of denial and failure to acknowledge the seriousness of the present. A mindless repetition of creeds and confessions is rarely sufficient in volatile times. Jeremiah faced precisely this crisis of vision when he refuted the people who could recite "The temple of YHWH, the temple of YHWH, the temple of YHWH!" but not see the train that was headed straight toward them. Finally, the memory of God's ancient acts of power can evoke bitterness if God fails to act in the present crisis. After all, what good is it to cling to a God who can help but chooses to do nothing?

It is likely that the people who prayed Psalm 74 included individuals from all of these camps. There were those who were fully cognizant of the danger they faced and chose to trust in the power of YHWH. There were those who denied the seriousness of the moment and clung to soothing words. And there were those who were embittered by God's failure to act and who flirted with practical atheism. For each set of voices the libretto begins the same, but the musical score differs. It will take a decisive awakening before all voices sing the same tune. That awakening will come, but not before enormous protest.

Three of the six potential songs of Zion found in the Psalter occur in Book Three: 76, 84, 87.[13] Although each psalm is distinct, their similar

---

[12] Mays writes that "God is told who he is in terms of title and its reality. . . ." (*Psalms*, 245).

[13] The remaining Zion songs are 46, 48, and 122 (cf. McCann, "The Book of Psalms," 648). Psalm 132 is also a candidate for this category. See Kraus, *Psalms 60–150*, 474–79; Gerstenberg, *Psalms, Part 2*, 368.

concerns allow them to be considered quickly together. *Psalm 76* celebrates God's presence in Jerusalem/Zion and the Deity's victory over
Israel's enemies. God is characterized as a roaring lion that routs all opposition,[14] who establishes justice and saves the oppressed (v. 9). While the
psalm is intensely focused upon Zion, its vision does not stop there—a
comment that is valid for all of the Zion songs. As the most sacred of
spaces, Jerusalem was the center from which blessing flowed to the rest
of the world (cf. Ezek 47). The reign of God, centered in Jerusalem, was
for the well-being of all of creation. Clinton McCann is correct in his assessment that "Zion functions in Psalm 76 as a symbol of God's sovereignty in all times and places. . . ."[15] The psalm offers a celebration to
the God who reigns from Zion on behalf of all the world.

　　Psalm 84 reflects on the beauty *(yyĕdîôt)* of YHWH's dwelling precincts
(v. 1). James L. Mays comments that the "appeal of the holy place is first of
all religious, not aesthetic."[16] Perhaps he is correct in the sense that not all
religious experiences happen in beautiful surroundings. The small, one-
roomed, weather-boarded church building that housed the congregation
from which I first heard the stories about Moses and Jesus that helped
shape my life certainly would not qualify as beautiful. But one should not
be too quick to draw a sharp line between religion and aesthetics. Among
many things, the keen attention to rhetorical crafting of divine oracles by
the prophets would caution against such a move. In this psalm, the poet
takes a break from the normal discourse of life to reflect on the order and
harmony—the beauty—that ensue from an encounter with God at
Zion.[17] Presence and place merge in such a meeting and the result is hap-
piness *(ʾasĕrê*—vv. 4, 5, 12). The psalm is bold in its acknowledgement of
God as king (v. 3) and also in its prayer for the earthly king *(mĕšîaḥ*—v. 9).
In fact, both the divine and earthly kings are called a "shield" *(mgn)*, highlighting a royal ideology that was introduced in Psalm 2 and will be taken
up in the final psalm of Book Three (89). In Psalm 84 the villager and pil-

---

[14] The nouns that are used to describe God's "abode" *(sukô)* and "dwelling place" *(mĕ
ʿônātô)* (NRSV) in verse 2 are used elsewhere to name the lair of lions (e.g., Pss 10:9 and
104:22, respectively).

[15] McCann, "The Book of Psalms," 980.

[16] Mays, *Psalms*, 274.

[17] This "break" could be quite literal if we take our cue from verses 5-7, which suggest a pilgrimage to Jerusalem.

grim, the birds of the air (v. 3), the king and YHWH are all connected in an exhilarating moment of bliss that concludes with the exclamation: "YHWH of Hosts! Blessed [happy] is the one who trusts in you!" (v. 12).

The difficulty of translating and understanding *Psalm 87* is almost universally acknowledged by its interpreters. For example, Kraus writes, "in this badly injured psalm the half-verses have been torn apart and senselessly coordinated."[18] He then offers a rearrangement of the text that he proceeds to interpret. Others retain the order of the Masoretic text but still acknowledge the psalm's interpretive difficulties.[19] For example, it is difficult to know the identity of the speaker in verses 4-5. It could be God, a prophet, or the personified city Zion. Still, some things seem more certain.

Mays suggests that the psalm treats two main topics. First, "Zion is the city of God," and second, "the city of God is the spiritual home for people who live in all nations."[20] The first two verses affirm God's attachment to Jerusalem with the singularly occurring statement: "YHWH loves the gates of Zion more than all the dwellings of Jacob" (v. 2).[21] These gates are part of the city that rests firmly on the holy mountain (v. 1). The mention of "holy mountain" evokes mythological thoughts of the cosmic mountain that stands at the center of the world. This is the place where creation began, a point of contact between the human and divine worlds, the place from which life-giving power and instruction flow outward to the rest of the world.[22] The second section of the psalm (vv. 3-7) would support this understanding with its universalizing claim that all people are children of Zion. Notably, among people specifically mentioned by the poet are Egypt (Rahab), Babylon, Philistia, and Tyre: historic enemies of Israel! These, too, are children of Zion and God's people. Zion and God's presence there are not simply for Israel, but rather for the well-being of the entire world.

---

[18] Kraus, *Psalms 60–150*, 184.

[19] McCann, "The Book of Psalms," 1023; Tate, *Psalms 51–100*, 387–88.

[20] Mays, *Psalms*, 280–81.

[21] McCann notes that the expression "gates of Zion" is unique to this text. "The Book of Psalms," 1024.

[22] See Jon Levenson's discussion of Zion as the cosmic mountain in *Sinai and Zion: An Entry into the Jewish Bible* (Minneapolis: Winston, 1985) 111–37. Comments by Marvin Tate (*Psalms 51–100*, 391) are also to the point.

This concentration of Zion songs in Book Three is striking given the stark admission of the Temple's destruction in Psalm 74. In light of these songs' high view of Jerusalem and God's special presence there, how should we construe the jarring acknowledgment of the holy city's decimation on the one hand and rapturous delight in Zion on the other? At least three possibilities come to mind.

First, one might simply ignore their canonical/story position and seek to understand them in light of a reconstructed *Sitz im Leben*. For example, some scholars have sought to relate Psalm 76 to a specific event, such as Sennacherib's invasion of Judah in 701 B.C.E., or a cultic enthronement festival of YHWH.[23] Additionally, Psalm 84 has been described as a pilgrimage psalm possibly sung en route to the autumn festival and various historical settings have been proposed for Psalm 87.[24] But such reconstructed settings for the psalms are always immensely tentative and rarely offer little help in reading them in their present location in the canon.

Second, one might propose that the association of Psalm 74, with its lament over Jerusalem's devastation, calls for the Zion songs to be read eschatologically. Despite all appearances to the contrary, the ebullient hope and enthusiasm of Psalms 76, 84, and 87 look to the future when Zion will indeed be the life-sustaining center of the world. There is much to commend this line of interpretation, and certainly the exilic and later communities of Israel would likely have heard these as eschatological yearnings.[25] However, the nagging question about this interpretive move— at least from the voices that narrate Israel's story in the Book of Psalms— arises from the quick lunge from the lament of Psalm 74 to the bold assertions of Psalm 76. Granted, one can respond by saying that this is typical of Israel's tenacity to hope in spite of adversity—a tendency that is displayed in so many of the biblical laments. But the enormous depth of pain voiced in the final psalms of Book Three (88 and 89) leads one to believe that there are unresolved matters yet to settle. The Zion songs seem premature.

I would suggest, then, that in the flow of Israel's story in the Book of Psalms (i.e., in their canonical/"narrative" context) these songs that are

[23] See Kraus's discussion of setting in *Psalms 60–150*, 109.

[24] See the discussion offered by Tate (*Psalms 50-100*, 355 and 388, respectively).

[25] This is essentially the tack that McCann, for example, takes ("The Book of Psalms," 979, 1013, and 1023).

so gloriously fixed upon Zion may be the ultimate denial of reality. They are the voice of the mother who refuses to believe the police when told that her son has been killed in a drive-by shooting. They are the denial of the patient who will not hear the doctor's one word diagnosis: "Cancer." They are desperate acts of world maintenance and will not become authentic expressions of faith—eschatological or otherwise—until the hideous bad news is finally and fully acknowledged. That necessary voice of acknowledgment comes in Psalms 88 and 89.

Among all of the voices that speak from the tortured and raw edges of life in the real world, *Psalm 88* is without equal. It is a desperate voice of enormous pain and, to draw on the psalm's own images, dense darkness. The psalm is the lament of an individual consisting primarily of a complaint, with only a slight nod toward petition (v. 2), and at best an implicit ray of hope (v. 1). The move to affirmation that is characteristic of so many of the individual laments (e.g., Ps 13:5-6) is excruciatingly absent in Psalm 88. The unresolved conclusion to the prayer has led Brueggemann to characterize the psalm as "an embarrassment to conventional faith."[26] Indeed it is, for here there is no happy ending.

Verses 1-2 constitute an address to God and a petition. Both verses are fundamental to the interpretation of the prayer. The clearest note of hope is sounded by the psalm in its opening line: "YHWH, God of my salvation." The two designations for the deity are in apposition. To speak of YHWH is to speak of salvation. That is the nature of Israel's God. Even more to the point, this is the language of an insider who has more than a passing relationship with God. The Holy One is addressed not merely as 'a saving God,' but "the God of *my* salvation." The "cry" (s^cq) that the psalmist sounds forth in verse 1 is anchored in the "cry" (s^cq) that the God of Abraham, Isaac, and Jacob heard in Exodus 3:7. The psalmist stands in solidarity with the people that God has delivered ($nṣl$—Exod 3:8) in the past. The psalmist asks only one thing: "Let my prayer come to you" (v. 2). There are no lengthy entreaties, renewed petitions, and pleas—only the hope engendered by a God who listens. But it is, at best, a muted hope that is offered by these opening lines.

---

[26] Brueggemann, *The Message of the Psalms: A Theological Commentary* (Minneapolis: Augsburg, 1984) 78. Brueggemann goes on to argue correctly that the psalm has a valuable, although uneasy, place in the life of believing communities.

Verse three states the crisis that will be elaborated throughout the rest of the prayer. Hear, YHWH, because, "My being has been satisfied with evil things, and my life has arrived at Sheol." The "satisfaction" *(śbᶜ)* of the psalmist is of a very different sort than the "satisfaction" *(śbᶜ)* that God gives to the earth and its creatures in Psalm 104:13. In the latter there is abundant life, but in Psalm 88 the specter of death hovers near. Verses 4-9a follow quickly and saturate this second major section of the psalm (i.e., vv. 3-9a) with the chaotic waters of death and desertion. To return to the rubric used earlier, the psalmist's problem is personal, theological, and social.

Personally, this tortured soul stares death in the face. The language of "death" *(mt*—v. 5), "grave" *(qbr*—v. 5), "pit" *(br*—v. 6), and "darkness" *(ḥšk*—v. 6) drapes the psalmist like a funeral pall. Whatever has taken hold of the poet is horrible beyond adequate description.[27] Theologically, the psalmist lays the blame at YHWH's feet, for the Deity is the one who has placed *(šît)* him or her in the pit (v. 6). It is God's wrath *(ḥmt)* that surrounds this sad singer (v. 7). Theological and social dimensions merge in verse 8 as the psalmist prays: "You have caused my intimate friends to be far from me." Forsaken by God and friends, the psalmist is left to face death alone.

Through a series of rhetorical questions, the next section (vv. 9b-12) reminds God of the finality of death. In the grave, the wonders of God are not experienced, reasons for praise no longer exist, and voices no longer sing to YHWH. The bitter anguish of the psalmist leads to this rhetoric of desperate persuasion, one that pleads to be remembered (cf. Exod 2:24) by God instead of being sent to the land of "forgetfulness" *(nšyh*—v. 12).

In the psalm's final section (vv. 13-18) the poet laments being completely rejected *(znḥ)* by and hidden *(str)* from God (v. 14). The psalm ends in a bleak acknowledgement: "You have caused my friend *(ʾhb)* and neighbor to be far from me; my intimate friend is darkness." There is no word of hope, no note of affirmation, no praise. There is only the inability to see one's way out of the cavern of misery.

Such language and theological reflection are hard. We in the Church do not deal well with them. We are much more inclined to silence such

---

[27] It is tempting to think only of a deadly illness when trying to account for the psalm's language, but Tate is likely correct in saying that "the metaphorical backdrop is wider than sickness and can encompass any severe distress or life-threatening situation" (*Psalms 51–100*, 401).

'outbursts' and resort to those absolute but vacuous categories of omni-science, omnipotence, and omnipresence.[28] Perhaps we need no more graphic reminder than Psalm 88 that all theology is ultimately and in-evitably contextual and that our efforts to draw upon universal axioms in order to speak soothing words of help and truth are doomed to failure. Marvin Tate wisely has written of Psalm 88 that

> this is a landscape which some have never known and perhaps never will. For others, however, its bleak features are well known because of journeys there. Some will know of it only as passing tourists, but others are long-time sojourners in it and know it well—too well.[29]

We do well to hear the voice of others who have walked where we have not walked and seen what we have not seen. Pastoral counselor Kathleen Billman is correct in saying that in order to help people find their voice we must make the commitment to "listen past the borders of our catego-ries, to communicate our valuing of what is waiting to be voiced, to learn a language that may be quite 'other' from our own. . . ."[30] In fact, we may discover that our own salvation lies precisely in allowing these un-settling voices to speak.

Psalm 89 is a puzzling text on a number of fronts. Its peculiar mix of hymnic (vv. 1-2, 5-18), oracular (vv. 4-5, 19-37), and complaint (vv. 38-51) elements has led to endless questions about the psalm's unity.[31] The jar-ring juxtaposition of the high claims for the Davidic monarchy in verses 19-37 and the anguished complaint of the demise of that very monarchy in verses 38-51 remains a paradox of the first degree. The precise histori-cal event that may have resulted in the demise of the Davidic monarchy remains uncertain.[32] These are but a few of the problems that have plagued

---

[28] For a review of the classical, and totally unsatisfying, ways of dealing with the-odicy see Thomas Oden, *Pastoral Theology: Essentials of Ministry* (San Francisco: Harper & Row, 1983) 223–48.

[29] Tate, *Psalms 51–100*, 405.

[30] Kathleen D. Billman, "Pastoral Care as an Art of Community," in Christie Cozad Neuger, ed., *The Arts of Ministry: Feminist-Womanist Approaches* (Louisville: Westminster/ John Knox, 1996) 31.

[31] See, for example, Kraus, *Psalms 60–150*, 201–2; Tate, *Psalms 51–100*, 413–16.

[32] See Tate, *Psalms 51–100*, 416–17, for a useful summary of alternatives that have been offered.

the interpretation of Psalm 89. Because these issues have received so much attention in the various commentaries, I will not rehearse them here. For this discussion I will treat the psalm as a whole with all of its tensions, despite its potentially complex literary history. Also, it is sufficient to note that whether the precise events that gave rise to verses 38-51 occurred before, at, or after 587 B.C.E., the location of these verses in the final form of the canon inevitably conjures up the fall of Jerusalem to Babylon at that time.

The psalm opens with a bold celebration of Yhwh's steadfast love (*ḥsd*) and faithfulness (*ʾmn*) (vv. 1-2) and concludes with a desperate query about what has become of these two divine attributes (v. 49).[33] That which seems undeniable at the beginning of this discourse is thrown into tortured questioning and becomes unbelievable at the end. The path between the beginning and end is every bit as twisted.

Immediately after the initial celebration of the Deity's steadfastness and faithfulness, the psalmist recounts an oracle about God's covenant with David (vv. 3-4). The oracle announces: "I will establish forever your offspring, and I will build generation after generation your throne" (v. 4). Immediately on the heels of this oracle a hymnic section (vv. 5-18) celebrates Yhwh's power as creator and sustainer of the cosmos. Verses 5-8 emphasize God's faithfulness as recounted by celestial regions, here the heavens (v. 5) and the divine council (vv. 5b-7) (cf. Ps 82). Verses 9-18 look down from the heavens toward the earth, where God's victory over Rahab and subsequent righteous and just rule are celebrated. Behind these verses, of course, lie ancient Near Eastern notions of a god who overcomes the primordial chaos to order the world and who is then acknowledged king in heaven and on earth (cf. vv. 9-11, 18).

At this point in the psalm, attention again returns to God's covenant with David (vv. 19-37). Thus, the cosmogonic section (vv. 5-18) essentially functions as an intercalation, piercing the discussion of David's rule with assertions about Yhwh's rule. Human and divine rule are interwoven by the psalmist and comment upon each other. Just as God rules over the cosmos, the Davidic monarchy rules over terrestrial arenas. In fact, God extends the divine power to rule over the sea (*ym*—v. 9) to the Davidic

---

[33] See McCann ("The Book of Psalms," 1034) for a concise summary of the dispersion of these key words throughout the psalm.

king whose hand is placed over the sea (*ym*—v. 25).[34] This is David's legacy, vouchsafed by YHWH's oath (v. 35).

The final section of the psalm (vv. 38-51) is an anguished complaint that is framed by the pained references to God's anointed who has now been passed over (*ʿbr*—v. 38) by God and is reproached (*ḥrp*—v. 51) by God's enemies. God has spurned *(nʾr)* the covenant with David (v. 39) and clothed him with shame (v. 45). The psalm concludes with imperatives that God remember the mortality of humans (v. 47) and the reproach of YHWH's anointed (v. 50).

Like Psalm 88, there is no happy ending. Or, as Tate observes, these two psalms "have no proper closure."[35] He continues by writing that Psalms 88 and 89 "do not end with domesticated consonance. In the long run, however, their dissonance may be a greater source of strength and comfort. Strength is not built on easy stories with happy endings."[36]

Preliminary Observations

The episode of Israel's story that is told in Book Three of the Psalms begins on slippery ground (73:2) and ends with David's crown *(nzr)* dishonored and lying on the ground (89:39). In spite of the intervening voices that sing of Zion's glory (Pss 76, 84, 87), the Davidic monarchy has fallen. This catastrophic episode is a graphic reminder that while bold voices of hope have their important place in the life of faith, they ring true only after a realistic assessment of the sociopolitical and theological landscape. No matter how well intended, naïve words of praise can function to numb the masses and legitimate the status quo. Brueggemann writes that

> where lament is absent, covenant comes into being only as a celebration of joy and well-being. Or in political categories, the greater party is surrounded by subjects who are always "yes-men and women" from whom "never is heard a discouraging word." Since such a celebrative, consenting silence does not square with reality, covenant minus lament is finally a practice of denial, cover-up, and pretense, which sanctions social control.[37]

[34] For a succinct summary of the many parallels between God's rule and David's rule in Psalm 89, see Tate, *Psalms 51–100*, 423.

[35] Tate, *Psalm 51–100*, 430.

[36] Ibid.

[37] See Walter Brueggemann, "The Costly Loss of Lament," in Patrick D. Miller, ed., *The Psalms and the Life of Faith* (Minneapolis: Fortress, 1995) 102. Brueggemann has ex-

This kind of situation is not far from the one that Jeremiah faced upon hearing the optimistic words of Hananiah, to which he responded:

> The prophets who preceded you and me from ancient times prophesied war, famine, and pestilence against many countries and great kingdoms. As for the prophet who prophesies peace, when the word of that prophet comes true, then it will be known that the Lord has truly sent the prophet (Jer 28:8-9; NRSV).

There comes a time when the boil must be lanced.

The hard and raw voice of pain can be neglected only at the expense of a community's well-being. Time and time again, the biblical traditions give privilege to the voice of pain. God heard the voice of Abel's blood crying (ṣʿq) from the ground (Gen 4:10), and the outcry (ṣʿq) of Israel in Egyptian bondage (Exod 3:7). Special protection is continually afforded the widow, orphan, and stranger (e.g., Deut 24:19-21; Lev 19:33). Older members of society who may no longer be able to work and contribute to the economic health of the community are to be honored (Lev 19:32). The biblical traditions invite those anguished people who have been locked outside of sacred doors to enter boldly and make their voices heard. Kathleen Billman and Daniel Migliore write that "the prayer of lament and protest provides a language of suffering missing in the language of the everyday as well as in the technical jargon of science. Lament is an indispensable vehicle to articulate the pain and outrage that would otherwise remain voiceless."[38] Failure to hear and welcome this voice is to hide behind the illusion that "all is well."

The perplexed and pained voices that frame Book Three of the Psalter (Pss 73, 74, 88, 89) expose naïve praise (Pss 76, 84, 87) as a grasping at straws in the wind. These voices of tortured realism admit to the authenticity of collapse. The world that once seemed so secure is now shattered. They are like the voice of the addict who finally hits rock bottom, who stares death in the face without the security of illusions, who in weakness finally finds the courage to say, "My name is _____ and I'm an alco-

---

plored this tendency extensively in his volume *Israel's Praise: Doxology Against Idolatry and Ideology* (Philadelphia: Fortress, 1988).

[38] Kathleen D. Billman and Daniel L. Migliore, *Rachel's Cry: Prayer of Lament and Rebirth of Hope* (Cleveland: United Church Press, 1999) 107.

holic." And ultimately, they are the voices that pave the way to healing and lay the foundation for authentic words of praise.

Canon and Congregation

To the extent that Loren Mead is correct that the Church is experiencing the collapse of one mode of existence (Christendom) and awaiting the emergence of a new mode, Book Three of the Psalter is roughly analogous. The collapse of the Davidic monarchy, the destruction of Jerusalem, and the exile were events that shattered the theological, political, and institutional landscape of Israel. In other words, there is a convergence of the Church's present situation and Israel's story in the Psalms. What might we make of this convergence?

It is worth noting that internal and external forces prompted the emergence of monarchy in Israel. The external forces, in particular the Philistines, are most typically cited. But the Book of Judges offers more than a few hints that internal tensions were moving the confederation toward change. The geographical isolation of the various tribes, inequitable distribution of resources, tribal jealousies, and conflicts all pulled at the fabric of the early tribal confederation (cf. Judg 5, 17-21).[39] To use the lenses of congregational studies, ecology and culture were involved in the appearance of monarchy. In the same way, internal and external forces were involved in the collapse of monarchy. The prophets were not loath to point out the internal shortcomings of Israel (cf. Jer 7) and the rise of the imperial powers of Assyria and Babylon provided immense external pressure. It is especially noteworthy that painful stories accompany both the emergence and collapse of monarchy, from the gang rape and dismemberment of the Levite's concubine (Judges 19) to the oppression and murder cited by Jeremiah (7:5-11). Pain gives birth to monarchy and eventually announces its death.

Israel's memory of monarchy, both in its beginning and its end, retains the memory of pain. The voices are not expunged from this incredible story. In fact, the voices of pain are most clearly heard at liminal moments—moments that might mean death, or birth, or both for Israel. These voices of pain come to us as sacred stories, as part of canon, or

[39] Bruce Birch, et al., *A Theological Introduction to the Old Testament* (Nashville: Abingdon, 1999) 216–18.

Scripture. As such, they urge us to give them their say as we ponder who we are as God's people and how to respond accordingly.

Because Israel's story remembers that internal and external forces were instrumental in the emergence and collapse of monarchy, accompanied by voices of pain, the lenses of culture and ecology provide a natural entry to consider voiced pain, Israel's story, and congregational life.

What are the internal voices that have been silenced for too long, the voices from within *congregational culture* that beg for a hearing? No doubt there are many, but I will comment upon three.

First, there is the *voice of the laity*. For many liturgical traditions the voice of the laity has been limited to the "script" provided by the worship bulletin or prayer book. Stand, sit, or kneel at the right time; sing at the right time; pray at the right time.[40] To put it another way, the clergy directs and the congregation performs. Such an arrangement need not be seen as inherently manipulative and may, in fact, be viewed as benevolent and wholesome. But comfortable relationships can conceal issues of codependency that gradually destroy the creative gifts of each party. Drawing on insights from family process, Mead describes clergy who are often "overfunctioners." He writes that

> In attempting to help someone out of a bad patch of one kind or another, the helper makes decisions or directs behavior that should be made and directed by the person in trouble. By rationalizing his or her actions as "help" for one who is "helpless," the helper only serves to create dependency and provide the person in trouble with an excuse to abdicate personal authority. . . . Continued over time, these patterns of behavior create a class of overfunctioners and an underclass of underfunctioners, and the conditions themselves become chronic and self-replicating.[41]

---

[40] I do not intend to denigrate the significance of liturgical actions by a congregation. Linda J. Clark, for example, has discussed the importance of hymn singing in congregations. She observes that "hymns both express and form faith" (Clark, "Hymn-Singing: The Congregation Making Faith," in Carl S. Dudley, et al, *Carriers of Faith: Lessons from Congregational Studies* [Louisville: Westminster/John Knox, 1991] 55). Hymns are constitutive, and that is no small matter. My point, though, is that in multiple congregations today there are non-clergy members who are capable of writing their own hymns instead of singing those handed to them by the clergy.

[41] Loren Mead, *Five Challenges for the Once and Future Church* (Washington, D.C.: Alban, 1996) 12.

In such a situation, a clergy member's need to feel useful and a parishioner's unwillingness, fear, or inability to make a stand mutually support one another. It is a stifling cycle that maintains the status quo.

Mead and others cite the increased role of the laity in carrying out the mission of the emerging Church.[42] William Diehl insists that "the mission field is right outside the doors of our congregations, and it is the laity who will have to be the missionaries. There is no other way open to the church."[43] Some clergy members no doubt will feel threatened or disoriented by the emerging voice of members in the congregation. Others may see it as a misguided example of the blatant spirit of individualism and repudiation of authority so characteristic of, especially, the United States.[44] But Psalm 88, the lament of an *individual,* is a poignant reminder that hard speech may be more indicative of the actual health of a community than the proscribed prescriptions offered by a religious elite. There is a theological warrant offered by Book Three of the Psalter to create the space and build the podiums for those who have been denied voice to rise and tell their own stories. Nancy Ammerman has commented that "for congregations . . . the most crucial resource is membership."[45] It seems a bitter irony that this 'most crucial resource' is routinely used but "kept in its proper place."[46]

Second, there is the *voice of women.* Despite the many gains made by women in the past two decades, the Church is still a bastion of patriarchalism. The silencing of women can be sanctioned officially, as was done

---

[42] E.g., Loren Mead, *The Once and Future Church* (Washington, D.C.: Alban, 1991) esp. 24, 35–37, 41–68; *Five Challenges for the Once and Future Church,* esp. 1–16; William Diehl, *Ministry in Daily Life* (New York: Alban Institue, 1996).

[43] William Diehl, *Ministry in Daily Life,* vii.

[44] McKinney and others write that "Perhaps more in North America than in other parts of the world, individuals in congregations have the strong sense that they *are* the church. This sense is affirmed more in some traditions than others, but even in religious bodies where connections are officially prescribed, there is a resistance to 'external' authority imposing its will on local communities of faithful people" (William McKinney, et al., "Resources," in Nancy Ammerman, et al., *Studying Congregations: A New Handbook* [Nashville: Abingdon, 1998] 132).

[45] Nancy Tatom Ammerman, *Congregation and Community* (New Brunswick, N.J.: Rutgers University Press, 1997) 346.

[46] I will have more to more to say about the role of the laity in the next chapter when I consider the democratization of leadership in Israel's story and in congregational life.

by the Southern Baptist Convention in its "Ahasuerus-like" move in 1998 when women were instructed to "submit graciously" to their husbands.[47] Large quarters of the Church still persist in their refusal to ordain women as clergy, citing the authority of Scripture or tradition, or both. But theology is never far removed from sociopolitical contexts, and the issue of power is always near the surface of these ecclesiastical debates. Mary Donovan Turner and Mary Lin Hudson have written that

> the control of power in relationship affects the voice and silence of each group within a system. One in power easily assumes the right to speak. Others are denied that right or must seek permission in order to be heard. In some cases, even when an oppressed voice speaks, especially without the permission of the powerful, that voice is ineffective, because the powerful cannot bear to hear it. Thus, the struggle for voice is not only a struggle to speak, but also a search for an audience to listen.[48]

In the meantime, the struggles persist, congregations languish, and gifts are wasted.

Indeed, there are times in the Church when women speak but are not heard. Patriarchal patterns of conducting business, deciding upon which programs should be undertaken, or who should teach in the religious education courses are well entrenched. Consequently, when women question, for example, the processes by which decisions are made, their questions may go unheard by males who assume the answer is obvious. Carol Gilligan has written that "the failure to see the different reality of women's lives and to hear the differences in their voices stems in part from the assumption that there is a single mode of social experience and interpretation."[49] Despite some shifts, that single mode of social experience and interpretation continues to be male. The inability to hear and appreciate the voices of women in our congregations is a further drain on the vitality of our religious communities.

---

[47] In the Book of Esther, King Ahasuerus sends a royal edict throughout the Persian Empire ordering that all wives should honor their husbands when, ironically, his own wife Vashti refused to do as the king ordered.

[48] Mary Donovan Turner and Mary Lin Hudson, *Saved from Silence: Finding Women's Voice in Preaching* (St. Louis: Chalice, 1999) 16–17.

[49] Carol Gilligan, *In a Different Voice: Phychological Theory and Women's Development* (Cambridge: Harvard University Press, 1982) 173.

Third, there is the *voice of victims*. Here lies the sordid side of silence. In commenting upon conspiracies of silence, Carl Dudley writes "rather than confront difficult situations, congregations often respond by denying the evidence and punishing those who present it."[50] As a result, victims of sexual harassment and violence can be stripped of speech. The recent revelations of sexual violence in the Roman Catholic Church reveal how long the confusion and shame suffered at the hands of a once trusted priest can go unspoken. And we need not think that violence is lacking in Protestant congregations. Marie Fortune begins her monumental volume, *Sexual Violence: The Unmentionable Sin,* with this telling observation, "For centuries the message has been effectively communicated: speak not about rape, incest, child molestation—especially in the Church. So the sin of sexual violence (and some even argue it is no sin) has remained unmentionable."[51] For a congregation to silence the voice of the victims, whether out of denial, embarrassment, or fear of legal actions, is to harbor a deadly cancer that eats away at the heart and soul of people created to bear the image of God and the Body of Christ itself.

Beth Tanner has offered a suggestive intertextual reading of Judges 19 and Psalm 88 that gets to the heart of sexual violence. The Judges text narrates the hideous tale of a Levite whose concubine is given to a violent crowd to spare the Levite shame and harm. She is called only a concubine and a woman, but never named. She is brutally raped by a gang of men throughout the night and is released at dawn to crawl back to the door that protected the Levite from the night's harm. When he opens the door and sees her lying there, his first words to her are the command, "Get up" (Judg 19:28)! The narrator then reports, "But she answered nothing." This nameless victim is also deprived of voice. Tanner suggests reading Psalm 88 as the woman's prayer. The psalm, of course, goes unanswered and the concubine dies. There is no happy resolution to the terror of these texts, but the pain of sexual violence is voiced by their presence in Scripture.[52] Tanner writes that "Psalm 88 and the unnamed Concubine stand as a connection to the senseless violence in our own world. And if for no other reason, these texts, then, belong in the canon—

[50] Dudley, "Process: Dynamics of Congregational Life," in *Studying Congregations,* 120.

[51] Marie Marshall Fortune, *Sexual Violence: The Unmentionable Sin,* xi.

[52] See Phylis Trible's treatment of Judges 19 in *Texts of Terror,* OBT (Philadelphia: Fortress, 1984).

to see that at least we are not alone with our questions and our outrage in the face of cruelty by humans and the absence of God."[53] To deny the outrage and to silence the pain of the victim is to perpetuate the sin that hides safely behind the doors of the Church.

In addition to internal voices that announce the collapse of old ways of existing (and implicitly announce new possibilities), external voices challenge previous, and perhaps current, assumptions about the Church's identity. One of the reasons that Israelite monarchy disappeared was that the world became too small for Judah to hide any longer and Babylon arrived at the gates of Jerusalem. Mead has argued that a key signal that the Christendom Paradigm has collapsed and a new Church is emerging is the shifting of the mission fields. "We now assume that the door of the church is a door into mission territory, not just a door to the outside."[54] There is no sacred barrier at the distant edges of the Empire. A brave, new world has arrived at the doorsteps of every congregation. I mention only three related external, or *ecological,* voices that announce the end of one era and the beginning of a new one.

First, there is the voice of the *diminutive world* in which we live. On this rainy fall day as I have sat in my Memphis home in front of my computer writing these words, I also have exchanged e-mails with my parents in Kentucky. I have found out that my father's biopsy procedure went well, and I have learned about the accidental death of a 1960s high school friend. I have read an on-line article from *The New York Times* about a serial killer terrorizing suburban Washington, D.C., and have made airline reservations to Toronto for later next month. I have checked websites for information on population growth, and corresponded with people from the midsouth to the northeast who serve with me on a committee. At one point I passed by our family's "bulletin board" on the refrigerator and saw "Cell Phone" listed at the top of our oldest daughter's Christmas wish list. Early this morning, as Federal Express planes zoomed overhead, I watched our youngest daughter drive to school by herself for the first time. There is no hiding from the outside world anymore. This exposure can be painful because it typically calls into question our own socially

---

[53] Beth LaNeel Tanner, *The Book of Psalms Through the Lens of Intertextuality,* Studies in Biblical Literature, 26 (New York: Peter Lang, 2001) 171.

[54] Mead, *The Once and Future Church,* 25.

constructed worlds by reminding us that there are other possible modes of existence. Quite simply, we are not alone.

Second, and related, North Americans are hearing the voice of *radical demographic shifts*. For example, from 1990 to 2000 Connecticut, Massachusetts, New Jersey, New York, Pennsylvania, and Rhode Island experienced a total population growth of 5.36 percent (47,909,201 to 50,474,842). However, the Hispanic population in these states grew 39.82 percent during the same period of time (3,732,566 to 5,218,734).[55] Specifically, Nancy Ammerman notes the population shifts in the Allston-Brighton, Massachusetts, area from 1970–1990 where the white population dropped from 95.7 percent to 72.8 percent and the Hispanic population rose from negligible to 9.2 percent.[56] Closer to my own home in Memphis, the Hispanic population in Arkansas grew from 19,878 in 1990 to an estimated 49,473 in 1998, making Arkansas the nation's leader in Hispanic population growth.[57] Amazingly, most experts on Hispanic population growth agree that official counts are far too low and that the actual numbers are much higher. Over the past four years, a thriving Hispanic congregation has blossomed at the end of my street. The need for bilingual voices in law enforcement, legal representation, medical and social services has by itself signaled the presence of "the Other" at our doors.

Third, there is the voice of a *different faith*. While many Hispanics have a Christian background, that is not the case with immigrants from other parts of the world. According to some counts there are currently ten million Muslims living in the United States, an increase of 25percent from 1989–1998.[58] That total compares with 15.3 million Southern Baptists. Given these numbers, the ongoing acts of violence in the Middle East (which most conservative religious people in the United States understand quite inadequately), and the events of September 11, 2001, it is understandable (and inexcusable) that religious intolerance is at a high. Recent statements by Jerry Falwell (Muhammad was a terrorist, "a violent man, a man of war") and Southern Baptist president Jerry Vines (Muhammad was a "demon-possessed pedophile") exemplify the dangerously paranoid

[55] "Latino Population Growth in the Northeast." www.lehman.cuny.edu.

[56] Ammerman, *Congregation and Community*, 15.

[57] www.usccr.gov/pubs/arsac/ch1.htm.

[58] "The World's Major Religions Changes," http://islamicweb.com.

side of groups frightened by different voices.[59] Of these Mead correctly writes: "These groups seem to be trying to rebuild a Christendom that is a 'holy club' of personal and family religious enthusiasm in, but not engaged with, the church's social environment."[60]

I have mentioned briefly only a few voices that call to congregations from within and without. Each, in its own way, conveys discordant tones of pain. There is the pain of the laity who sense their baptized vocation of offering ministry but are restricted by clergy. The voice of women laments the ecclesiastical strictures that deny them the chance to fulfill completely their divine mandate to bear the image of God to the rest of the world. Tragically, there is the literal pain that arises from the cry of the violently abused victim. From without comes the pained sense of loss that can arise upon discovering that our own socially constructed worlds are much smaller and far more tentative than we ever imagined. Not only do we no longer know the neighbors on the street, but we no longer speak the same language, say the same prayers, or sing the same hymns. There is the painful sense of the loss of the old community.

The predictable tendency is for congregations to attempt to silence or deny the existence of painful voices. Israel tried both. The people clung to the hopeful words of prophets like Hananiah (Jer 28), while they beat and publicly humiliated Jeremiah (Jer 19:1-2), tried him on the capital offence of treason (Jer 26), and threw him into the solitary confinement of a cistern thinking he would die (Jer 38). In the end, Babylon breached the walls of Jerusalem. Congregations will be no more successful than Israel. Sooner or later, in one way or another, lament will make its voice heard. The challenge for congregations is to give that voice its full audition, to embrace its painful tune, and to discover with Israel that the lyrics of sad singers are also lyrics about our future.

Summary

In this chapter I have argued that the episode of Israel's story narrated by the voices in Book Three of the Psalter is an episode about col-

---

[59] These statements were cited in a report of a Memphis gathering of Muslims, Jews, and Christians who voiced their opposition to Falwell and Vine. See Jacinthia Jones, "Leaders Join to Oppose Falwell on Islam," *The Commercial Appeal,* October 8, 2002, Section B, 1.

[60] Mead, *The Once and Future Church,* 41.

lapse. It is framed by perplexed and painful voices that will not be silenced (Pss 73, 74, 88, 89). To be sure, not all voices sing the same sad song and opt for lighter lyrics (Pss 76, 84, 87). But these voices proved false in the same way that Hananiah's hopeful words were eventually proven not to be the Word of the Lord. Israel's future would lie at the end of the road that led straight through the heart of lament.

Likewise, the time of the Church "to do business as usual" has come to an end. Although some ecclesiastical hierarchies will persist in singing Songs of Zion, the dirges from within and without congregations will eventually prove the poor timing of these light tunes. If the Church is to learn anything from Israel's story in the Psalms, it is time to listen to voices that sing sad songs, to encourage them, to create the space in our congregations for these voices to sing, and to honor them. "What might happen if these people come to voice?" some might question. Perhaps nothing less than the salvation and rebirth of the Church. But that is the topic of the next chapter.

5

Reemergence

salms 88 and 89 signaled both an end and a beginning. Monarchy as a form of social self-determination and self-rule was a thing of the past. Israel, as a geopolitical wheeler and dealer, had been dealt the card of death. Although monarchy and self-determination would continue to function as powerful ciphers for disoriented Israel's future theological and socio-political reflection, the actual institution was as dead as Saul after falling upon his own sword. The ending of Book Three admits that death.

At the same time, full and honest acknowledgement of death opens many powerful doors to the future. Death, that most liminal moment of all, has a way of directing one's mind and imagination to incredible possibilities. When death is fully accepted, alternative modes of reality never before considered begin to come into focus. The ending of Book Three also opens the door to new possibilities.

To be sure, that which a people deems to be new always and inescapably draws from the past. That will be the case as Israel's story in the Psalms responds to the crisis that gave rise to the laments in Psalms 88 and 89. To recall James Sanders's words, "One observation that impresses itself time and again in the study of history is that in crisis situations only the old, tried and true has any real authority."[1] But a return to the past

---

[1] James Sanders, "Adaptable for Life: The Nature and Function of Canon," in James Sanders, *From Sacred Story to Sacred Text* (Philadelphia: Fortress, 1987) 21.

has soteriological power only after the utter reality of the crisis is fully confessed. That is why Songs of Zion between Psalms 74 and 88–89 sounded inauthentic. However, the desperate admission of collapse sounded by the end of Book Three adds a very different quality to the glances toward the past and the praise that characterize Books Four and Five of the Psalter. We might call that quality honest hope.

Honest hope acknowledges the reality and pain of loss. It does not hide from the present moment, no matter how bleak or challenging the immediate landscape may appear. It also searches its canonical memory for ancient voices that speak with authenticity and familiarity to address a desperate community in a threatening context. Honest hope understands that this search will not yield a simple program that can merely be replicated in a radically changed environment, and admits that ancient voices will likely have to learn a new language. Nonetheless, honest hope is grounded in canonical memory. It is precisely this kind of faith that Israel musters in the conversation that takes place in Books Four and Five of the Psalter.

Conversation

The first sound uttered by *Psalm 90* in Book Four is subtle but immensely significant: "A prayer of Moses, the man of God." Form critics have typically heard this voice, but usually have paid little attention to it. Hans-Joachim Kraus, for example, comments upon the uniqueness of the superscription (i.e., it is the only psalm title to mention Moses), and then largely ignores it in his exegesis of the psalm.[2] In contrast, people who have explored the canonical shape of the Book of Psalms have given more heed to this unique utterance. Gerald Wilson, for example, observes that this is the first of seven references to Moses in Book Four compared to only one such reference elsewhere in the entire Psalter (Ps 77:21).[3] It is as if David, whose name appears only twice in Book Four, has been "replaced" by Moses.[4] Clinton McCann is surely correct in his judgment that this emphasis upon Moses is not coincidental and that it "takes the reader

---

[2] Hans-Joachim Kraus, *Psalms 60–150: A Commentary*, trans. by Hilton C. Oswald (Minneapolis: Fortress, 1989) 215ff.

[3] Gerald Wilson, *The Editing of the Hebrew Psalter*, SBLDS (Chico, Calif.: Scholars Press, 1985) 187. The seven references are Psalms 90:1; 99:6; 103:7; 105:26; 106:16; 106:23; 106:32.

[4] David's name appears in the superscriptions of Psalms 101 and 103.

back to the time of Moses, when there was no land or temple or monarchy."[5] The first note sounded in Book Four, then, is in response to the painful questions that concluded Book Three. "Remember," it says, "there was a time before David. There was a time in the wilderness when land was only a promise. But it was also a time when God was known in powerful and foundational ways. It was the time of Moses. Remember."[6]

As the first unit of Psalm 90, verses 1-2 make two powerful assertions.[7] First, the Lord has been Israel's "refuge" *(mā'ôn)* for generations. The relationship between God and Israel is long and deeply textured. Second, in a move that carries the reader to a time much earlier than even Moses, this Lord was God long before the "mountains were born." Israel's identity is tied up with the enduring being of this God who existed before the establishment of the ordered world. These verses invite Israel to reflect upon the disorientation of Babylonian Exile—the "new wilderness"—from within a cosmic framework. "Moses" reminds this new generation that their well-being is grounded in the eternal creator.

The next two units (vv. 3-6, 7-12) set Israel's tangible existence in marked contrast to the enduring quality of God's being. They protest that human life is short and generally lived under divine anger. In a mode typical of Israel's sages, the brevity of life is illustrated by the ways of the created world: grass that is green in the summer morning can be wilted and brown before the sun sets (vv. 5-6). Life in the wake of Babylonian triumph is like wilted grass. Such a life, reasons the poet, could only result from divine anger.[8]

The association of divine anger with human calamity is, and should be, problematic to us. Yet, despite all of the dangers with such an arrangement—and there are many—this voice from the Psalms attests to some

---

[5] J. Clinton McCann, "The Book of Psalms," *New Interpreter's Bible* (Nashville: Abingdon, 1996) 1040.

[6] Mosaic authorship of the psalm is, of course, not the question here and is no more defensible than Davidic authorship of the David psalms. Marvin Tate offers a useful summary of reasons that scribes associated the psalm with Moses (*Psalms 51–100,* WBC [Dallas: Word Books, 1990] 438).

[7] McCann identifies verses 1-2, 3-6, 7-12, and 13-17 as the basic units of the psalm ("The Book of Psalms," 1041).

[8] The prophet of the exile, whose voice comes to us in Isaiah 40–55, also employs the image of wilted grass to describe the exiles' plight. Cf. Isaiah 41:6-8.

important convictions. Israel refuses to grapple with the Babylonian Exile exclusively on political terms. The loss of king and country was not merely a matter of Babylon's military superiority, strategic planning, or even Israel's bad luck. Israel's theologians would not concede that "secular" powers had done them in. Even in an event as gargantuan as Judah's decimation, God had to be involved in some manner. It is this conviction that leads to the basic petition of the psalm's final unit.

Verses 13-17 are punctuated with a series of imperatives: "turn," "repent," (v. 13); "satisfy" (v. 14); "make glad" (v. 15). Boldly the psalmist stakes out hope in a cosmic God who can "turn" and "repent" *(šûb; nāḥam)* in the same way that the creator of all peoples did with the Ninevites in the Book of Jonah (3:9-10).[9] Even closer to Israel's memory was Moses' petition after Aaron and the people's construction of the golden calf in Exodus 32. In that moment of divine wrath *(ʾap)* when God wanted to destroy the people (Exod 32:10; cf. Ps 90:7, 11), Moses petitioned God to turn and repent *(šûb; nāḥam;* Exod 32:12) with the result that God repented (Exod 32:14). In Psalm 90, Moses once more asks for divine favor that will at the least return some semblance of balance to life (v. 15). The psalm ends with a petition that the work of human hands might be "established" *(kûn).* Intriguingly, this verb can be used to talk of God's "establishment" of the world (e.g., Ps 24:2) or, in its nominal form, to speak of the earth's "foundations" (e.g., Ps 104:5). This cosmogonic echo forms an inclusion with the cosmogonic images that open Psalm 90 and embrace Israel and its exilic crisis within a universal frame of reference. This final petition is, essentially, a plea to the God of all creation for some sense of permanence.

Psalm 91 sounds the next voice in Book Four. Because of certain associations with Psalm 90, a few comments about this text are in order. Form critical discussions about the psalm's proper genre and its original setting in life are complicated and divergent.[10] However, its literary context and content present suggestive interpretive possibilities.

For one thing, the psalm lacks a superscription in the MT.[11] This lessens the sharp break between Psalms 90 and 91 and allows them to be heard

---

[9] The same Hebrew verbs are used in Jonah 3:9-10 that are used in Psalm 90:13.

[10] For a good summary of the form critical discussions, see Tate, *Psalms 51–100*, 450–53.

[11] The LXX provides a Davidic superscription, however. This may reflect later scribal tendencies to attribute to David psalms that had no title in the MT. See Tate, *Psalms 51–100*, 451.

closely together. Then, there are other features that connect the two psalms. Psalm 90:1 referred to God as Israel's dwelling place *(mā'ôn)* and 91:9 uses the same word. Also, the petition of 90:14 for God "to satisfy us" is answered by 91:16 where God (it seems) promises "to satisfy [the people] with length of days."[12]

Psalm 91 consists of two basic parts: verses 1-13 and 14-16. The first section reflects upon God's beneficent protection offered to those who trust in the Almighty. In these verses, Israel is typically addressed in the second person and God is described in the third person (e.g., vv. 3-4). As Roland Murphy comments, "The hostile powers are described in traditional metaphors: snares, plague, night terrors (demons), arrows, sun rays (v. 6), lions, and serpents."[13] The addressee is well protected!

Verses 14-16 have the character of a divine oracle. Here God is no longer the object of narration. Instead, God directly promises those who love the Almighty and know the divine name deliverance *(plṭ*—v. 14), security *(śgb*—literally, "set on high," v. 14), divine answers, or response *('nh*—v. 15), rescue and honor *(ḥlṣ; kbd*—v. 15), satisfaction and salvation *(śb'; yš'*—v. 16). Divine help is more than equal to the potential dangers that the psalmist may encounter.

Together, Psalms 90 and 91 are thoroughly theocentric. They acknowledge human frailty and transience on the one hand, and the sufficiency of God's presence and deliverance on the other. They peer backward to a time when life was lived day by day in a constantly threatening wilderness. There were no kings and standing armies. It was God and Moses who taught, who provided, who led. Together, Psalms 90 and 91 point the way that a different Israel in a different wilderness will have to take. Like the recovering alcoholic, kingless Israel will have to take life one day at a time ("teach us to count our days"—90:12; NRSV) and trust in a Higher Power (91:1-2). Here in this wilderness of withdrawal Israel will name that Power in no uncertain terms.

Gerald Wilson has reasoned that Book Four is the editorial center of the Book of Psalms. He persuasively argues that the emphasis upon God as refuge and the stress upon the reign of YHWH in Book Four respond to the dilemma voiced by Psalm 89.[14] We have heard the affirmation of God

---

[12] See McCann, "The Book of Psalms," 1047.

[13] Roland Murphy, *The Gift of the Psalms* (Peabody, Mass.: Hendrickson, 2000) 130.

[14] Wilson, *The Editing of the Hebrew Psalter,* esp. 215.

as refuge in Psalms 90 and 91. However, the proclamation of YHWH's reign that comes in rapid succession in Psalms 93 and 96–99 begs for more scrutiny.

These psalms have been the center of considerable controversy in the history of interpreting the psalms. No small part of this debate is due to Sigmund Mowinckel's contention that these texts figured prominently in an annual Israelite enthronement festival where YHWH was "made" king anew.[15] At the center of the discussion is the expression YHWH *mālak* (Pss 93:1; 96:10; 97:1; 98:6 [with a slight variation in the formula]; and 99:1). Mowinckel understood this cultic cry as central to the hypothesized enthronement festival and contended that it is best translated as "YHWH has become king!" Not many scholars today would follow Mowinckel completely down the paths he blazed, and most scholars prefer to translate the Hebrew expression as either "YHWH is King," or "YHWH reigns!"[16] However, Walter Brueggemann recently has given fresh attention to Mowinckel's understanding of the power of speech. In particular, he argues that praise is not merely responsive but is also constitutive.[17] Quite simply, language has the power to "make" and to "unmake" social worlds.[18] For some modernists who have allowed the force of rhetoric to be eclipsed by an epistemology based solely upon "observable fact," this claim is controversial and perhaps lost. But for anyone who has ever walked into a worship setting with pain gnawing at her very being, who, after participating in the liturgy, felt the mysterious release from anguish, talk about the power of words will not be wasted. Words have power, especially those that are anchored in One not always clearly perceived in desperate moments. The shout "YHWH reigns!" is not simply a wish; it is the faithful affirmation of a reality that slowly and powerfully takes hold. I will offer a few brief comments on two of these psalms to illustrate the depth and power of these daring words: Psalms 93 and 96.

[15] For English readers this presentation is most accessible in Sigmund Mowinckel, *The Psalms in Israel's Worship*, 2 vols., trans. D. R. Ap-Thomas (Nashville: Abingdon, 1962).

[16] For example, Tate, *Psalms 51–100*, 472. See also James L. Mays, *The Lord Reigns* (Louisville: Westminster/John Knox, 1994) 13.

[17] Brueggemann, *Israel's Praise: Doxology against Idolatry and Ideology* (Philadelphia: Fortress, 1988) esp. 1–28.

[18] See, among the many discussions available, Peter Berger's comments on language in *The Sacred Canopy: Elements of a Sociological Theory of Religion* (Garden City, N.J.: Doubleday, 1967) 3–28.

Psalm 93 opens with the exclamation "Yhwh reigns!" and immediately depicts the divine king clothed with majesty and strength (v. 1). The testimony that follows links the establishment *(kûn)* of the world, the establishment *(kûn)* of God's throne, and the enduring character of Yhwh (vv. 1b-2). Unlike David's reign, Yhwh's kingship coincides with the foundation and duration of the ordered world. Then with threefold repetition, the next words depict the roaring of waters (literally "rivers") and evoke the notion of the cosmogonic battle between the creator god and chaos (v. 3).[19] In the next breath the psalmist insists "More than the voices of the many waters; majestic—more than the breakers of the sea; majestic on high is Yhwh!" (v. 4). Finally, the psalmist concludes by announcing the firmness of Yhwh's statutes or decrees *(ʿēdōt)* along with Yhwh's enduring being.

This brief hymn is stunning and profound. It is stunning as a voice from the chaotic wilderness of post-587 b.c.e. that refuses to submit to seemingly overpowering forces. It is profound because at the same time this voice does not deny the reality of chaos screaming so loudly that rational thought is difficult. The roaring sea is real and fearsome. To the dismay of many confronted by the face of evil, the establishment of the world by and the rule of Yhwh do not eliminate threat.[20] But the psalm is clear to affirm that God's majesty outstrips the ferocity of the roaring waters. Intriguingly, the poet insists that Yhwh has established firm statutes *(ʿēdōt)*. The Hebrew word typically refers to divine instructions to humans that are to be enacted in the social realm of Israel (e.g., Deut 6:17). In the cosmogonic context of Psalm 93, however, these statutes may also extend to Yhwh's instructions to the roaring waters to stay in the bounds assigned to them.[21] In fact, James L. Mays has perceptively observed that

[19] In Ugaritic myths, Nahar ("River") and Yam ("Sea") are parallel word pairs and personify the chaos that Baʿal overcomes to establish the world.

[20] The classic study of the continued existence of chaotic forces after the initial ordering of the world is Jon Levenson's volume, *Creation and the Persistence of Evil: The Jewish Drama of Divine Omnipotence* (San Francisco: Harper and Row, 1988). More recently, see Carol Newsome's insightful discussion of God's speech from the whirlwind in the Book of Job. At one point she writes that "God not only has to persuade Job of the fundamental reliability of the structures of creation but also simultaneously has to persuade him to recognize *the presence of the chaotic as a part of the design of creation*" (emphasis added). Carol Newsome, "The Book of Job," *New Interpreter's Bible*, vol. IV (Nashville: Abingdon, 1996), 614.

[21] Although different words are used, this notion is found in Psalm 104:9.

here "the ordering of the world and the ordering of society are expressions of one and the same rule."[22] There is hope in this voice, then, that as surely as the cosmos holds together the social fabric that constitutes the warp and woof of Israel will also hold.

Psalm 96 is typically understood as a hymn. Various proposals for the psalm's structure have been offered, but the basic division presented by Marvin Tate is useful.[23] Verses 1-6 exhibit the typical hymnic formula of an imperative to praise (vv. 1-3) followed by a reason for praise (vv. 4-6). The pattern is loosely repeated in verses 7-13.

The opening verse commands "all the earth" to sing a new song to YHWH. Hence, the psalm is universal in its scope. There is considerable discussion among scholars as to what precisely is meant by the expression "new" song. The main possibilities tend to be new in the sense of a special song written for a cultic event; new in the sense of a song that responds to a recent historical event; or new in the sense of an eschatological song that envisions a new future.[24] Many people would agree that these possibilities are not necessarily mutually exclusive.[25] Strictly speaking, a new song is "new" for any given audience only once. After that its newness fades into the familiar tones of an old song. At this point, a song's newness arises from hearing it in a changed context. This observation would caution against equating the adjective "new" with the moment of this hymn's composition and instead commend hearing the text of Psalm 96 in the changed rhetorical situation of exile. The newness of the song arises from the dissonance of its lyrics when compared to the plight of the Judean exiles. Such songs, when offered in full and honest acknowledgment of pain, are counter texts that refute the claims of oppressive powers and offer new visions of hope. The psalm is eschatological in that it conflicts with the present claims of the world; yet, eschatology is always intimately concerned about the present. Familiar songs in changed contexts offer a unique collision of the past, present, and future that imbues them with the character of newness.

[22] James L. Mays, Psalms, Interpretation (Louisville: Westminster/John Knox, 1994) 301.

[23] Tate, Psalms 51–100, 512–15. For a more nuanced proposal see Gerstenberger, Psalms, Part 2, and Lamentations, Forms of Old Testament Literature (Grand Rapids: Eerdmans, 2001) 187.

[24] See McCann's discussion in "The Book of Psalms," 1064–65.

[25] For example, McCann, "The Book of Psalms," 1065; Tate, Psalms 51–100, 513.

The three plural imperatives that introduce Psalm 96 demand the audience to "sing" *(šîrû)*. It is in the human, embodied act of singing with other humans that new possibilities for Israel are unleashed. Singing is inherently a communal act. Even a performance oriented society such as ours where professionals sing and the masses are entertained can't eliminate the communal nature of singing. Drivers sing with their radios. Concert goers mouth, if not actually give voice to, the lyrics sung by performers. Even people who claim not to be able to sing will find themselves tapping a foot or finger, or nodding in time with the song. Singing is an infectious activity that will not leave one alone until it has worked its musical magic. The threefold command to sing is immediately followed by an imperative to "declare" or "rehearse" *(spr)* the glory of YHWH (v. 3). The singing and telling of the worldwide community in Psalm 96:1-3 constitute a powerful rhetorical move that helps crack the door to a new world and energize the people to step forward.

The first three verses of the psalm also direct its message to two audiences: "all the earth;" and "YHWH." Like most of the psalms, this song is both social and theological. Without the theological dimension the psalm would be little more than wishful thinking. The reason for praise that is offered in verses 4-6 anchors the psalm in the creative power of God: "YHWH made the heavens" (v. 5b). As the Creator, the gods of the peoples are proven to be "worthless" or even nothing at all *(ʾĕlîlîm—v.* 5a). As the Creator, it is YHWH who is surrounded by majesty and honor (v. 6). At the risk of being reductionistic, it is possible to summarize Psalm 96:1-6 by saying that YHWH is "song-worthy" because YHWH is the Creator.

Just as the first major unit began with three imperatives instructing all the earth to sing, the second major unit (vv. 7-13) begins with three imperatives that demand the clans or families of the peoples to "ascribe" *(hābû)* to YHWH "glory and strength" (vv. 7-8a). In further acknowledgement of YHWH's might, the people are demanded to bring a gift and to enter YHWH's courtyards in order to worship the royal Creator (vv. 8b-9). A central part of their homage is the affirmation by the nations that "YHWH reigns!" (v. 10). The reign of God is immediately linked to the Creator-King's establishment of the earth and the royal responsibility to judge the citizens of the universal kingdom with "evenness" or "equity" *(mêšār)*. The prospect of fair and equitable judgment by the divine king evokes cosmic rejoicing as the heavens, the earth, the sea and its creatures, the field and its inhabitants, the trees in the forest burst out in rejoicing (vv. 11-12). This raucous hymn concludes with a restatement of the reason for such joy: ". . . because [YHWH] comes to judge the earth. He will judge the world with righteousness, and the peoples with his fidelity" (v. 13b).

From this brief discussion of Psalms 93 and 96, several important themes can be identified. YHWH is the one who makes and/or establishes the heavens and earth. This establishment is accomplished in such a way that the earth will not be moved. Further, the creative power of YHWH shows the other gods to be worthless, if not powerless. As Creator, YHWH is deserving of honor and majesty and acknowledgment as the universal king: "YHWH reigns!" The divine rule is characterized as righteous and fair. It is a rule that the elements of the natural world recognize and exult in. It is a rule that the psalms insist all peoples of the earth to acknowledge and then urge them to respond by offering reverence and worship.

Before listening to other voices that speak from the exilic episode of Israel's story, it may be helpful to bring together some of the ideas that have emerged from the speakers so far. Importantly, they all speak in full awareness of the bitter severity brought on by the Babylonians. In this they are like Jonah's song of thanksgiving uttered from the belly of the great fish (Jonah 2). It is hard to deny reality while floating in gastric juices! So far, the psalmists of Book Four have looked to a time before Israel had their own land. In a previous wilderness, under the leadership of Moses, YHWH ruled. While on the land, Davidic monarchy had its possibilities. But now, no longer in the land, Israel remembered and again acknowledged the universal scope of YHWH's reign. Israel's future would lie in the relinquishment of its claims of autonomy and self-rule and its ultimate trust in the creator of all the earth. Utter trust in YHWH engenders hope and a new zest for life. It gives birth to the imagination to see new possibilities.

The theological notes sounded by the psalmists so far carry with them certain sociopolitical implications. The poets don't advocate or spell out a particular form of social organization, but their insights would have incredible significance for whatever form of government the people might construct. Perhaps most significantly, all of creation—both nonhuman and human—are the results of God's creative power and are called upon to acknowledge YHWH's rule. There is a radical democratization in this acknowledgement that places heaven and earth, tree and wave, fish and cattle, Judean and Babylonian "shoulder to shoulder" as God's subjects.

All social and ecological hierarchies are called into question upon affirming ultimate devotion and allegiance to YHWH. In addition, the characterization of YHWH's rule as righteous and fair for all of the earth's creatures, humans included, is profound. Any form of social organization that people might undertake that would lose sight of God's insistence upon righteousness and equity for all of creation would be far, far less that what these psalms envision.

To be sure, the theological claims and the social possibilities offered by Psalms 90, 91, 93, and 96 run counter to Israel's experience of exile. They are eschatological in the sense that they yearn for a time when life corresponds to their claims.[26] Or perhaps another way to view the claims of these psalms is to see them as the projection of an alternative vision. To the degree that a projected vision is compelling, people internalize parts of the vision and begin to live and act accordingly. Consequently, the vision offered by these psalms has the potential to initiate the actual construction of a new, alternative reality.[27] I will pursue this line of thought at more length as we listen to the next voice that I will call upon in the narration of Israel's story in the Psalms.

Psalm 104 is a magnificent hymn that meditates upon God's creative power and the world that God's power brings about. Although there are a number of ways to think about the psalm's structure, style and content support this arrangement: verses 1-4: theophany in the heavens; verses 5-9: establishing the earth; verses 10-18: life-giving waters; verses 19-23: night and day; verses 24-30: divine care for all of God's works; and verses 31-35: YHWH's glory and humanity's sin.[28]

The first unit opens with an imperative for the psalmist to render praise to YHWH: "Bless, O my life, YHWH!" (v. 1a).[29] The psalm moves

---

[26] This insight is especially underscored in McCann's discussion of the enthronement psalms (see, for example, "The Book of Psalms," 1053).

[27] See Peter Berger, *The Sacred Canopy;* Peter Berger and Thomas Luckmann, *The Social Construction of Reality* (Garden City, N.J.: Doubleday, 1966).

[28] The comments on Psalm 104 that follow have been shaped considerably by Walter Harrelson. See especially his article "On God's Care for the Earth: Psalm 104," *Currents in Theology and Mission* 2 (Fall 1975) 19–22.

[29] This expression occurs as an introduction in the Psalter only in Psalms 103 and 104 and provides the entrance for a fruitful discussion on the juxtaposition of the two psalms. I will not pursue those possibilities here, but see the suggestions by McCann, "The Book of Psalms," 1096.

quickly to offer reasons for God's praiseworthiness. Characterized largely by the use of present participles, YHWH is the one clothed with glorious splendor and light (vv. 1b and 2a). God stretches out the heavens as if they were a gigantic tent, and upon the upper waters lays the foundation beams for the divine palace (vv. 2b and 3a). The clouds serve as YHWH's conveyance, while the wind and lightening function as messengers (vv. 3b and 4). Cosmogonic images of making the heavens, exercising control over the waters and the thunderstorm, and of palace-building underscore the majestic power of God as creator that the rest of the psalm will carry forward.

In narrative-like fashion, the next unit (vv. 5-9) moves spatially from celestial regions to the earth.[30] With this shift of scenery also comes a grammatical shift from the use of participles to finite verbs. "[YHWH] has established the earth upon its foundations so that it shall never move" (v. 5). Intriguingly, the poet maintains that even "the deep" *(tĕhôm)* issues from YHWH as an initial covering for the earth (v. 6). At YHWH's "battle shout" the waters flee up the mountains and down the valleys to the place that has been assigned for them (vv. 7-9).[31] It is noteworthy that the deep is not eliminated, but rather restricted by boundaries established by YHWH. Even the *tĕhôm* has its proper place in God's good world.

Verses 10-18 are introduced by the grammatical shift to a participle and a change in content. After ordering the chaotic waters, the poet shifts attention to life-sustaining waters. The unit offers a panoramic view of those who benefit from the gift of water. Every wild animal—wild asses (v. 11), birds (v. 12), cattle (v. 14), gigantic trees in which storks build nests (vv. 16-17), mountain goats, and rock badgers—all of these benefit from the abundance of water. In this unit comes the first of only three references to humans in the psalm. Because of the rain, the earth produces bread and wine for food, and oil for the skin (vv. 14b-15). The psalmist even reflects on the joy that human life possesses as a result of the divine gift of water (v. 15a).

---

[30] Compare, for example, the narrator's comment in Genesis 11:5. "And YHWH *went down* to see the city and the tower that the humans had built."

[31] Both the NRSV and the NIV translate *gaʿărātĕkā* as "your rebuke." A. Caquot suggests that the shout is like the one of a "fierce warrior who 'cries out' in anger to drive away his enemies." See A. Caquot, *"gaʿar"* in TDOT, eds. G. Johannes Botterweck and Helmer Ringgren, trans. John T. Willis and Goffrey W. Bromiley (Grand Rapids: Eerdmans, 1978) 51.

Verses 19-23 shift from terrain to time. The moon and sun mark off night and day, affording both wild animals and people their secure times. While people sleep, lions hunt in the evening and are even assisted by God. With the rising of the sun, lions sleep and people work. It is important to emphasize that elsewhere in the psalms lions are depicted as ferocious creatures that are metaphors for the wicked enemy (cf. Ps 17:12). Here, however, they have their place in God's world just as the deep has its place. Lions are not eliminated but rather assigned their proper time and place (cf. Job 38:39-40). The psalmist envisions an orderly coexistence between the human and animal realms.

Verses 24-30 are introduced by a pause, or break in narration. In wonder and astonishment the psalmist addresses YHWH directly: "How many are your works, O YHWH!" (v. 24a). Then, in amazement the poet glances to the sea that is filled with innumerable creatures. It is a place of mystery where there are creatures that are small and large—even Leviathan![32] Yet it is also a place where ships filled with people can sail as long as the ships stay above the water and Leviathan remains beneath.

The final section (vv. 31-35) prays that God may continue to delight in the works of creation in full awareness that the Creator could bring an end to the ordered world if the cause should arise. And, in a move that has stunned many interpreters, the poet recognizes that the one thing that can place the well-ordered world in danger is the presence of sinners. Although YHWH provides water to sustain human life, along with times and places to work, the poet knows that humans are quite capable of using divine gifts foolishly and thereby can tear at the fabric of the world's harmony. So, the psalmist petitions that sinners be obliterated from the earth (v. 35).[33]

---

[32] On Leviathan see especially Isaiah 27:1 where the aquatic creature is described as a monstrous dragon. A similar image also appears in Job 41. Both texts are indebted to the mythic notions of the chaotic waters that are defeated by the creator god in primeval time. In view of these references it is not wise to think of Leviathan in Psalm 104:26 as a domesticated playmate. Once again, the psalm affirms that chaos has its proper place and role.

[33] Some commentators have concluded that verse 35 is so out of character with the rest of the psalm that it must be a secondary addition. For example, see Charles A. Briggs, *The Book of Psalms,* International Critical Commentary (New York: Charles Scribner's Sons, 1917) 339. On the other hand, John Calvin rightly saw that the final verse was an integral part of the psalm. See John Calvin, *Commentary on the Book of Psalms,* trans. James Anderson (Grand Rapids: Eerdmans, 1949) 171.

As a whole, Psalm 104 is a remarkable portrayal of the orderliness of the world that is abundantly attended to by YHWH. Life is, or at least can be, good. Walter Brueggemann has discussed the hymn as a psalm of orientation, and pointed out how such psalms can be used socially as a form of manipulation and control.[34] Much depends, of course, upon the rhetorical situation in which the psalm is heard and Brueggemann is quite aware of this.[35] Kings can chant the psalm much as incumbents in an election chant slogans in order to stress to the populace that all is well. But, opponents might use the same libretto to mount a challenge to the desired office by saying, "Would that things were really this nice!" To a suspicious reader, there are clues (admittedly inconclusive) that would support the opponent rather than the incumbent.

For one thing, there is the admission by verse 35 that sinners do exist. Clearly, there are some problems, or at least potential problems, out there in the world. For another thing, the psalm itself borders on the utopian. It raises the question, "When was life ever *this good?*" That is Walter Harrelson's point when he asks "Where are all those waters, where is all that idyllic life of ordered existence in troubled Palestine?"[36] These questions are all the more poignant when heard from the specific rhetorical situation of the exile. Clearly, the psalm cuts across the grain of lived experience. What do we make of this?

I will offer two complementary responses. First, grounded in theories of the sociology of knowledge, the psalm can be understood as an intentional projection of an alternative world. If the projection "takes hold," then it is appropriated and reappropriated by the society.[37] To the degree that the projection is internalized by the society, then the social world is shaped by the vision. When the projected vision is radically at odds with life as experienced, as Psalm 104 was for a devastated exilic community,

---

[34] Walter Brueggemann, *The Message of the Psalms: A Theological Commentary* (Minneapolis: Augsburg, 1984) esp. 25–28, 31–33.

[35] See, for example, his excellent discussion of Psalm 37 in Brueggemann, "Psalm 37: Conflict of Interpretation," in Patrick D. Miller, ed., *The Psalms and the Life of Faith* (Minneapolis: Fortress, 1995) 235–57.

[36] Walter Harrelson, *From Fertility Cult to Worship* (Missoula: Scholars Press; reprint ed.; New York: Doubleday, 1969) 91.

[37] Peter Berger describes this as the process of externalization, objectivation, and internalization. See *The Sacred Canopy*, 3–28.

then the projected vision becomes subversive and struggles to upset the oppressive status quo.[38] Second, Rolf Jacobson has used insights from cognitive dissonance theory constructively to consider the clash between expectations and experience. When a psalm "doesn't fit" life as it is currently known, then the "human mind will seek to resolve this dissonance: either by changing cognitions, adding new cognitions, or changing attitudes."[39] That is, dissonance can be the spark that ignites hope. The abrasive fit of Psalm 104 and the Exile, the mix of hymnic praise with horrific pain, can become caustic to the oppressors. In the end, hymns can "hem in" the captors.

Along with Psalm 104, *Psalms 105 and 106* conclude with the shout "Praise Ya!" *(haleluyah)*. As Gerald Wilson observes this grouping is not likely accidental, and together the three psalms close Book Four. While Psalm 104 reflects upon the universal sovereignty of YHWH and the orderliness of the cosmos, Psalms 105 and 106 narrow the focus as they consider God's work with the people Israel. The move is like the one in the Genesis narrative as it shifts from YHWH's concern with the peoples of all the earth in Genesis 11 to God's dealings with the ancestor Abraham in Genesis 12. Psalm 104 locates Israel's particular story in Psalms 105 and 106 within a universal framework.

Psalms 105 and 106 are both historical psalms that recount God's relationship to Israel, and they invite consideration together.[40] At the same time, the two psalms differ considerably in the way they remember the covenantal relationship between YHWH and Israel.

In hymnic fashion *Psalm 105* opens with an imperative to "give thanks to YHWH" (v. 1a). This is followed by a litany of imperatives that instruct Israel to "call," "make known," "sing," "make music," "talk," "praise," "search," and to "seek" (vv. 1b-4). Perhaps the most significant impera-

---

[38] I have argued this point before in "The Rhetoric of Creation: Psalm 104 as a Subversive Text," SBL presentation to the Book of Psalms Group (New Orleans: 1990).

[39] Rolf Jacobson, "Burning Our Lamps With Borrowed Oil," in Stephen Breck Reid, ed., *Psalms and Practice: Worship, Virtue, and Authority* (Collegeville: The Liturgical Press, 2001) 97.

[40] See McCann, "The Book of Psalms," 1103–4. On these and the other "historical psalms" (Pss 78 and 136) see also Walter Brueggemann, *Abiding Astonishment: Psalms, Modernity, and the Making of History*, Literary Currents in Biblical Interpretation (Louisville: Westminster/John Knox, 1991).

tive, though, is the one that begins verse five: "Remember," *(zikrû)*. This psalm is about memory—Israel's memory and YHWH's memory. While Israel is commanded to remember YHWH's wondrous deeds, signs, and judgments (v. 5), it is God's memory of the covenant with Abraham that drives Israel's story (v. 8).

In keeping with the character of Book Four to respond to the questions raised by the end of Book Three, the covenant tradition singled out by the psalmist is the Abrahamic and not the Davidic covenant. Just as the beginning of Book Four reaches back to the era of Moses, the ending of the Book delves deeply into Israel's election traditions to a time much earlier than David.[41]

An important part of this covenant tradition involves the land. Between the promise of land (v. 11) and the gift of the land (v. 44) the psalm selectively rehearses Israel's story by highlighting the ancestral wandering (vv. 12-15), Israel's descent into Egypt (vv. 16-25), the Exodus (vv. 27-38), and the wilderness wandering (vv. 39-42). The poet signals Israel's movement from the wilderness to the land by mentioning for the second time YHWH's memory: "Because he remembered his holy word, and Abraham his servant" (v. 42).

The psalm is entirely positive in its retelling of Israel's story. Importantly, throughout the psalm God is the subject of nearly every verb. The poet does not speak much of the people's response. The possession of land was not of their own doing but was grounded entirely in the memory, the grace, and the power of YHWH.

Tantalizingly, however, just before the final imperative to praise God, the psalmist claims that the land was given to the people "in order that they might keep his statutes, and his instructions they might observe" (v. 45). The pattern is similar to the one in the Exodus narrative, where God frees the slaves first, and then presents instruction at Sinai. The decalogue itself recounts the same sequence: "I am the YHWH your God, who brought you out from the land of Egypt, from the house of slavery. There shall not be for you other gods over me" (Exod 20:2-3). Legislation follows liberation. Israel is freed from human bondage to serve YHWH.

---

[41] As noted above, if Psalm 104 is kept in view with Psalms 105 and 106 the conclusion to Book Four pushes back to primeval moments long before there was an Israel and certainly long before there was a David.

Similarly, in the view of Psalm 105, Israel is given the land in order to keep God's statutes and instruction and thereby to serve God.[42]

Psalm 106 begins with the command to "Praise Ya!" followed by the same imperative to "Give thanks to YHWH!" that opened Psalm 105. Similar to Psalm 105, Psalm 106 also acknowledges the might of YHWH (v. 2a). And like its predecessor, Psalm 106 contains the key word "remember" *(zkr)* three times (vv. 4, 7, and 45). Psalm 106 is also keenly interested in memory. But these similarities only combine to underscore how much Psalm 106 is a reverse image of Psalm 105.

In one breath the psalmist observes "Happy are those who keep justice and do righteousness all of the time" (v. 3), and in the next demands "Remember me, O YHWH" (v. 4a). The shift from bold affirmation to petition suggests a gap between verses 3 and 4, and indeed, the rest of the psalm makes that quite clear. The situation of the people is far from "happy." The reason is clearly stated in verse 7: "Our ancestors in Egypt did not pay attention to your wondrous deeds, they did not *remember* [*zkr*] the abundance of your steadfast love [*ḥesed*]" (v. 7a). Near the outset of the psalm, we know that any remedy for the people's lack of memory will lie in YHWH's act of remembering. This is further reinforced by two occurrences of the word *šākaḥ*: "forget." The people "hurried, they forgot [God's] works" (v. 13) and "they forgot the God of their salvation" (v. 21).

In light of the people's forgetfulness, it is little wonder that the recital of Israel's history in Psalm 106 is entirely negative. From the exodus, through the wilderness wanderings, and even after entering the land, the forgetful and rebellious character of the people landed them in dilemma after dilemma. In spite of all of this "[YHWH] remembered, for them, his covenant, and was compassionate because of the abundance of his steadfast love" (v. 45a).

The ending of the psalm is an urgent petition for YHWH to save the people and to gather them from the nations (v. 47a). This petition is also an acknowledgment that the only source of deliverance that Israel can rely on lies in YHWH. Earthly princes and kings won't do. Human efforts will fall short. Only the God who has heard the cries of the people in the past, who remembers, and who acts with compassion and enduring love

---

[42] McCann also notes that grace precedes demand in this psalm ("The Book of Psalms," 1106).

can be counted on in the present moment of catastrophe. In a fitting admission that there is such a One, Book Four ends on a note of affirmation: "Praise Ya!"

Together, Psalms 105 and 106 present the goodness of God and the faithlessness of the people. When taken with Psalm 104, the ending of Book Four proclaims that YHWH is Creator, Redeemer, and Sustainer. From the disaster of the Exile, Israel looks back to what it has known so well and remembers once again. Israel's past has always belonged to YHWH, and so will its future.

Book Five of the Psalter is the longest, containing 44 psalms (107–150). The voices that narrate this episode in Israel's story give witness to a flurry of activity and sentiments. In many ways, Book Five is about *the possibility of movement*—physical, social, psychological, and theological movement. Indeed, one of the hallmarks of redemption and freedom is permission to move from one place to another. There are risks that come with movement.[43] But the only alternative is the same one taken by the servant in Jesus' parable who hid the master's money in the ground (Matt 25:14-30). With movement come risks, but also new possibilities.

Psalm 107 opens the final episode of Israel's story in the Book of Psalms and is intimately connected to the concluding voice of Book Four. There the psalmist had petitioned, "Save us, O YHWH our God, and *gather* [*qbṣ*] us from the nations" (Ps 106:47). Psalm 107 responds, "Let the redeemed of YHWH speak—those redeemed from the hand of distress. From the lands he *gathered* them [*qbṣ*]—from the east, from the west, from the north and from the south" (vv. 2-3).[44]

Verses 4-9 speak of people who are wandering about in the desert wastelands, perhaps having taken the wrong route *(tʿh)*. Hungry and thirsty they cry *(ṣʿq)* to God who responds by directing them to the correct route ("a straight way"—v. 7). The images of wandering in the desert, hungry and thirsty, evoke Israel's paradigmatic wilderness trek: the Exodus experience. While the verses need not refer to the Exodus, in the exilic context the image of release and guidance would be particularly powerful.

---

[43] While working on this chapter, my oldest daughter totaled her car in a traffic accident. Fortunately, no one was seriously injured but I have been reminded anew of the risk that mobility brings!

[44] On the many other connections between Psalms 106 and 107 see McCann, "The Book of Psalms," 1116.

Verses 10-16 focus upon prisoners who are shackled in darkness. Their plight is said to be a direct result of their rebellion against the "words of God" (v. 11). Still, they cry to God who leads them out of darkness and imprisonment (vv. 13-14). Verses 17-22 concern the foolish, or sick, who have approached "the gates of death" through their iniquitous actions. These, too, cry out and are saved and healed. Verses 23-32 graphically depict sea-goers that are caught in a terrifying storm. The ferocity of the storm is reminiscent of the opening chapter of Jonah.[45] In their fear they cry out and God brings them out of their distress (v. 28).

Verses 33-43, and especially 39-41, speak of the power of God to effect reversals in ways that are evocative of the song of Hannah (1 Sam 2). Especially noteworthy is verse 40 where God "pours out contempt upon the nobility, and makes them wander in confusion [*tōhû*—cf. Gen 1:2] where there is no way." People in power and position find themselves powerless and displaced but the needy are "set" or "placed" (*śîm*—v. 41).

The psalm is filled with motion. People move from the deadly wilderness to inhabited places, from prison cells to freedom, from sickness to wholeness (this too is a physical "move"), and from threatening waves to placid seas. Socially, the psalm envisions an exchange of power as nobles are cast into the chaotic wasteland and the distressed are firmly established. Psychologically, the psalm is punctuated by the exchange of distress for delight. And theologically, the psalm calls for the people to see that YHWH is intimately involved in their plight and not removed from their concern. The *hesed,* or steadfast love, of YHWH surrounds (vv. 1, 43) and punctuates (vv. 8, 15, 31) the many calamities endured by Israel. Israel's salvation lies not in the power of the social elite, but in YHWH. As James Mays rightly observes:

> What sets the *hesed* of the LORD in motion in every case is the cry to the LORD in trouble. The psalm sees the *hesed* of the LORD manifest in salvation completely in this way. It elevates the prayer for help, the voice of dependence on God, to the central place in the relation to God.[46]

The only hope for movement of any kind in the exile lies in YHWH.

---

[45] Compare also the scene in the gospels where the disciples are terrified at the storm on the sea and cry out to Jesus in their fear (Mark 4:35-41; Matt 8:23-27; and Luke 8:22-24).

[46] Mays, *Psalms,* 347.

At the heart of Book Four lie sixteen remarkable Psalms: 119–134. If for no other reason, they are noteworthy because of length. Psalm 119 is the longest single psalm in the Psalter, and Psalms 120–134 are all titled "Song(s) of Ascents" and constitute the largest single collection of psalms outside of the Davidic groupings. While there are eleven Korah psalms (42; 44–49; 84–85; 87–88) and twelve Asaph psalms (50; 73–83), these groups are broken while the Ascents psalms are contiguous. At the very least, the duration of these psalms signals our attention. Just like the change of pace in narration from summary to elaboration signals the reader that the implied author is saying something important, the length of Psalm 119 and the grouping of the Ascents Psalms 120–134 urge the reader to slow down and pay attention. Yet, these psalms are noteworthy for reasons that exceed their length.[47]

As is well known, *Psalm 119* is an acrostic (i.e., alphabetic) poem. The psalm has twenty-two strophes, each consisting of eight verses. In the first strophe each verse begins with *ʾaleph*, the first letter of the Hebrew alphabet. Each line in the second strophe begins with *beth*, the second letter of the alphabet, and so on. Some translations, the NIB for example, indicate this by printing the name of the appropriate Hebrew letter at the beginning of each strophe. The subject of each unit of the psalm is Torah, with practically every verse using either the word Torah or one of seven other synonyms for Torah. As has frequently been observed, the psalmist seeks to say everything that can be said from (using English letters) A to Z about Torah.[48]

Beyond the alphabetic scheme, the progression of the psalm's content is not well understood. The first two strophes mention the word "way" (*drk*—vv. 1, 9) in their opening verses—a favorite theme of Israel's sages (e.g., Prov. 2:20). Further, that Psalm 119:9 is concerned about teaching youth *(nʿr)* additionally reminds the reader of the instructional material in Proverbs 1–9 that was specifically directed toward younger members of Israelite society. On the other hand, many of the strophes are strikingly reminiscent of the laments found elsewhere in the Psalter and petition God for help (e.g., vv. 17-24; 15-32; et al.). Other units exult in an

---

[47] Ironically, the length of these texts and the purpose of this project precludes a detailed discussion of these psalms. Brief remarks will have to suffice.

[48] For example, McCann, "The Book of Psalms," 1166.

almost intoxicated manner in the Torah (vv. 97-104). As the psalm's discourse about Torah moves through the alphabet, it holds together an amazing range of human situations and emotions. All of life, contends the psalmist, is best approached through an unflinching Torah piety.

It is important to underscore that this psalm is about the possibility of movement. There is movement through the alphabet—from *ʾaleph* to *tav* (A to Z). There is movement from subject to subject. There is movement from lament to praise. In the view of the psalmist, Torah is not static but rather dynamic and on the move. This understanding of Torah is especially significant for Israel in the Diaspora.

The fifteen Psalms of Ascents are as varied in content as the subjects in Psalm 119. The title "Ascents" *(maʿălôth)* is related to the Hebrew verb *ʾalah* that means "to ascend" or "to go up." Although the precise meaning of the noun *maʿălôth* is not clearly understood, many scholars take it to refer to pilgrimage.[49] Hence, these psalms may represent songs that were sung by pilgrims of the Diaspora who made their way back to Jerusalem for religious festivals. They are songs for people on the move.

This grouping of Ascents psalms is notable because of the many literary forms within it. There are psalms of complaint (120, 130), assurance (121), hymns (122, 132), confidence (123, 125, 131), thanksgiving (124, 125, 129), instruction (127), etc.[50] Generally, each psalm is brief, which has given rise to the plausible suggestion that they may have been easily memorized.[51] This feature would have commended their use for pilgrimages where the use of written texts would have been awkward.

This grouping of psalms is also remarkable for its frequent references to Jerusalem and Zion. Jerusalem is named five times in three psalms (122, 125, 134). Zion is named seven times in as many psalms (125, 126, 128, 129, 132, 133, 134). More oblique references to Jerusalem include "house of the Lord," "gates, walls, or towers," "house of David," "dwelling place," "holy place," "house," and "city" and occur at least twelve times in four psalms (122, 126, 132, 134). Among these psalms, 122 and 132 stand out.

Psalm 122 falls logically into three sections: verses 1-2, 3-5, and 6-9 (cf. NRSV). The opening of the psalm clearly depicts pilgrimage: "[to] the

---

[49] For the various possibilities that have been suggested see Hans-Joiachim Kraus, *Psalms 1–59: A Commentary,* trans. Hilton C. Oswald (Minneapolis: Fortress, 1988) 23–24.

[50] For example, see Gerstenberger, *Psalms, Part 2,* 317–77.

[51] See McCann's comments, "The Book of Psalms," 1176.

house of YHWH—Let us go!" It is a journey that calls forth joy and gladness. The psalmist ignores the spatial and temporal distance between verses 1 and 2. That is, there is no clue in the psalm about how far the poet traveled and how long the journey took. This ellipsis tends to focus all attention upon the destination of the journey: Jerusalem. In fact, Mays says that Psalm 122 "serves as a song of arrival."[52]

The second section (vv. 3-5) offers two reasons for pilgrimage. The first reason is explicit, and the second implicit. The people "go up" *(ʿlh)* to Jerusalem "to give thanks to the name of YHWH" (v. 4), and then to receive "judgment" or "justice" (*mišpaṭ*—v. 5). This section mentions David, but not so much as a yearning for a return to monarchy as for the benefit that monarchy was supposed to have provided: justice for all of the people.

The final unit (vv. 6-9) commands the people to pray for Jerusalem's well-being. Actually, the verb in verse 6 that is typically translated "pray" (NIB, NRSV) is *šaʾălû* and almost always means "to ask" or "inquire." It is, for example, the verb that is used in Psalm 137 when the Babylonian captors "ask" the captives to sing songs of Zion (137:3). While all petitions directed to God are prayers in some sense of the word, not all prayers are petitions. Since to ask or inquire is almost always to seek that which one doesn't have, the use of *sʾl* in 122:6 may point to the tenuous nature of Jerusalem's well-being and to the less than firm establishment that was announced in verse 3. In fact, such would have described precisely Jerusalem's situation during and after the exile. The unit ends with the psalm's second reference to the "house of YHWH" (vv. 1, 9). Although the house of David was mentioned in the psalm's middle verse (v. 5), it is surrounded by the dual references to YHWH's house. As Clinton McCann has seen, whatever can be claimed for the house of David in this psalm is derivative.[53] Ultimate authority resides in YHWH and YHWH's reign.

Psalm 132 is a jarring and perplexing voice in the Psalter's narration of Israel's story. It is the longest of the psalms of Ascents, and therefore stands out. Also, like no psalm since 89 this voice calls attention to David.[54] It is not surprising, therefore, that Psalm 132 is frequently listed among the Royal

---

[52] Mays, *Psalms*, 392.

[53] McCann, "The Book of Psalms," 1183.

[54] Two psalms often designated as Royal Psalms come between Psalm 89: Psalms 101 and 110. However, neither focuses as explicitly upon David as Psalm 132 does.

Psalms.⁵⁵ The text seems to fall neatly into two main sections: verses 1-10 and 11-18. The first unit tends to be a prayer and the second a response.⁵⁶

The psalm begins with an imperative for YHWH to remember the past efforts of David to locate a place for YHWH to dwell (vv. 1-5). Quickly the psalmist shifts to the present and speaks of a dual pilgrimage: that of the people to YHWH's dwelling place and that of YHWH's trek to the divine place of rest (vv. 7-8). The psalm is about movement and rest. However, past and present are merged in the references to the ark that David brought to Jerusalem (2 Sam 6) and to David as YHWH's anointed one (cf. 2 Sam 7). McCann rightly captures this merger in his comment that the "pilgrims to Jerusalem understood their journey as being analogous to David's earlier journey to Jerusalem with the ark; they, too, are accompanied by the presence of God. . . ."⁵⁷

YHWH's speech in verses 14-18 is important. God announces the divine intention to rest or settle *(nûaḥ)* in Zion forever. In response to the anguished query at the end of Psalm 89, YHWH assures that both Zion and David have not been forgotten. However, the fulfillment of the pledges to YHWH's anointed lie in the future. With the use of imperfect verbs, the psalmist signals that YHWH *will* cause a horn to sprout for David, and *will* clothe David's enemies in shame (vv. 17 and 18).

These high claims for Zion and David sound odd in the wake of the Babylonian devastation of Jerusalem. But the abrasiveness between text and context is central to interpreting the psalm in its canonical location. There can be no denying of calamity. But what of the future? Here the psalm sounds forth. As Mays has seen, the psalm is both "the voice of prayer and the proclamation of hope. In it, pilgrims hear that there will be—it is the word of the LORD—a horn and a lamp for David, there, in Zion."⁵⁸ As McCann notes, some may have heard this voice as affirming a return to the Davidic monarchy as it was in the past. But more sober and realistic listeners seem to have heard this threefold cord of YHWH, David, and Zion as a reference to God's relation to the entire people. Psalm 105:15 would surely suggest as much.⁵⁹ There "anointed ones" and "prophets"

---

⁵⁵ For example, Kraus, *Psalms 1–59*, 56.

⁵⁶ McCann, "The Book of Psalms," 1211.

⁵⁷ Ibid., 1212.

⁵⁸ Mays, *Psalms*, 412.

⁵⁹ McCann, "The Book of Psalms," 1212–13.

are parallel terms, and both seem to refer to Israel's ancestors, Abraham, Isaac, and Jacob. Increasingly, then, David is democratized and YHWH's pledge to David is heard as the divine pledge to the religious community Israel. Periodically and purposefully these people leave the Diaspora and travel to the cradle where they were nurtured in their infancy. The ancient claims associated with David are no more a private arrangement between God and an individual. The existence of a dispersed people is at stake. Consequently, the tenacious memory of David and Jerusalem anchors them wherever they live, and together a scattered and diverse community affirms its identity as God's chosen and anointed people.

It is suggestive, I think, that the lengthy discourse upon Torah in Psalm 119 and the Ascents psalms 120–134, with their focus upon pilgrimage to Jerusalem, are juxtaposed in the Psalter. In the second century B.C.E. Ben Sira subsumed Wisdom under the heading of Torah, and located the residence of Torah in Jerusalem (Sir 24). Although the conversation in Book Five of the Psalter is not as explicit, the sequential voices of Torah and Jerusalem are akin to the linkage of Torah and Jerusalem in Sirach. To live in the Diaspora is to live with Torah in hand and Jerusalem in view. To meditate upon and live by Torah is inescapably to remember Jerusalem. To journey to Jerusalem is unavoidably to encounter the judgments and justice that lie at the heart of Torah and to carry them back out into the world.

The singer of *Psalm 137* also holds together the memory of Jerusalem and the exercise of justice. It is a hard psalm and many people find it offensive because of its concluding section that desires vengeance upon the Babylonians, young and old. Indeed, the psalm should not be embraced too easily and quickly. It is to be reserved for those who have experienced unimaginable horror and carnage. Behind this voice lies the memory of Jerusalem under siege and starving people. The Book of Lamentations captures this dreadful memory with the line, "The hands of compassionate women have boiled their own children; they became their food in the destruction of my people" (Lam 4:10, NRSV). How does one respond to such a memory? Simply to turn and walk away would feed the cancer of hate that eats away at the soul. McCann writes that "the worst possible response to monstrous evil is to feel nothing. What *must* be felt—by the victims and on behalf of the victims—are grief, rage, outrage. In the absence of these feelings, evil becomes an acceptable commonplace."[60] The voice behind Psalm 137 chooses to feel—not in isolation, but in brutal conversation with God. This is a voice that seeks to face horrendous reality theologically. For this one, to remember Jerusalem is to remember YHWH and the justice of YHWH. The psalmist casts the pain and horror of life at the feet of God, who is the ultimate administrator of justice.

The Psalter ends on a resounding note of praise. *Psalm 145* introduces this jubilant chorus with the line, "I will exalt you, my God the King; I will bless your name forever" (Ps 145:1). In keeping with the basic tenor of Books Four and Five, God is acknowledged to be King. The next five psalms begin with the imperative to "Praise Yahweh!" The reasons for praise vary from "doing justice" (146:7), "building Jerusalem" to "giving food to cattle/animals" (147:2, 9). The entire cosmos is invited to join in praising YHWH (148) and the human community is encouraged to spare no means for offering praise (150). Fittingly, the final word in Israel's story in the psalms is, "Praise YHWH!" (150:6).

Again, the place in the conversation at which these voices of praise are sounded would guard against hearing them as naïve optimists. They come after the bitter collapse of monarchy (Ps 89) and the nightmarish memory of carnage in Jerusalem (Ps 137). Indeed, many of these voices are spoken in remote places far removed from Jerusalem. As such, they are voices that cut against the grain of experienced reality. But therein lies their power. Words of dissonance can be subversive words that eat away at powers that oppress, in order to engender hope.[61]

Preliminary Observations

The conversation in Books Four and Five of the Psalter is one of honest hope. That is, these voices own up to the loss of land and life that the Babylonian Exile brought. At the same time, these are voices that refuse to knuckle under to the chaos of destruction and deportation. In the final analysis, this is a conversation that seeks to frame the horror of the present within the memory of ancient traditions.

Book Four in particular remembers God's presence with Moses, Abraham, and the very origins of the world. The loss of the Davidic mon-

---

[60] McCann, "The Book of Psalms," 1228.

[61] Again, see Jacobson, "Burning Our Lamps with Borrowed Oil," 96–97.

archy is cast against the backdrop of a cosmic God. Israel's dilemma is thus set within a universal framework that has a place and time for the whole world, even the *těhōm* (deep) and lions that threaten humankind. On the one hand, this care that God exhibits for the whole of creation can be disconcerting for some. To affirm that God is the creator of and caregiver for all of the world and its creatures "decenters" any special interest group. The special claims of faith, denomination, or sect suddenly stand challenged by the overarching admission that everything that moves and breathes belongs to God. To acknowledge that YHWH reigns inevitably leads to a democratization of power. Human and institutional hierarchies fall and all people live under the reign of God. It is little wonder that religious communities have either ignored creation theology, or attempted to domesticate it so as to legitimate one religious regime or another.

On the other hand, to acknowledge God as Creator can be a source of immense hope for people who are oppressed. The prophet who uttered the words contained in Isaiah 40–55 understood this well, and drew extensively from Israel's creation traditions (cf. Isa 40:12-31). A God that can tend *těhōm* and lions is more than capable of tending a defeated Israel. And, if the deep and lions have their place in God's ordered world, then Israel too can be assured that it has a place. The demise of the Davidic monarchy does not eliminate the ancient bond between God and Abraham, Isaac, and Jacob. Within the grand sweep of time and space, Israel has a place.

If God is the creator of the entire world, then Book Five rightfully sees that Israel has the hope of movement. To be sure, this movement must honor the territorial claims of other peoples. But the Diaspora will not mean disintegration. Jerusalem will continue to function powerfully as a physical presence and as a symbol of God's special relationship with Israel. As Psalm 104 claims, there is a time for lions to sleep and for people to move about. Similarly, there will be those special times when Israel can move from dislocation to its sacred center in which praise abounds and from which justice flows.

Although especially associated with Jerusalem, God is present with the people wherever they may travel through the divine gift of Torah. Torah is dynamic and on the move with the people. On the one hand, to meditate upon Torah is to remember Jerusalem. On the other, to pilgrimage to Jerusalem is to meet Torah. This special association of Torah and

Jerusalem is comparable to the frequent descriptions of God as both transcendent and immanent. The instruction of YHWH is not limited to Jerusalem and is therefore available for God's people wherever they live. However, the association of Torah and Jerusalem in Book Five of the Psalter (and Sir 24) maintains that there is a palpable dimension of Torah experienced in this sacred center called Zion.

Finally, there is the subversive edge of Israel's praise. Like the songs of Paul and Silas from a Philippian jail (Acts 16:25-40), hymns can loosen chains of imprisonment. Honest praise presents an alternative to grim surroundings, evokes faith and actions that slowly, but powerfully, eat away at oppressive powers that feel they hold every card. Honest and realistic praise subverts old worlds of despair and opens the door to new worlds of shining possibility.

Canon and Congregation

The crisis that Judah suffered at the hands of the Babylonians could well have spelled the end of this unique people. Indeed, that is essentially what had happened to the Northern Kingdom, Israel, approximately one hundred and fifty years earlier when the Assyrians laid waste to Samaria. But the displaced Judeans found the resources to survive.

No doubt, considerable external forces that had not been available for the Northern Kingdom aided the survival of its Southern counterpart. The Assyrians practiced a two-pronged deportation policy that not only removed the Israelites from their native soil, but also replaced those carried away with people from other regions. There was a wholesale shuffling of the cards, so to speak. In addition, there is little evidence to verify that the deported Israelites were able to establish viable communities. The Babylonians, however, tended to remove only the upper echelon of a subjugated society and to settle them in reasonably intact communities on foreign soil (see Ps 137 and Ezek 1). Little intentional effort was made to resettle a conquered territory, and there seem to have been few barriers to impede social interaction among the Babylonian exiles. It is also significant that the Assyrian Empire retained its imperial hegemony over the ancient Near East for roughly one hundred years after taking the Northern Kingdom. Babylon, however, gave way to the Persians before fifty years had elapsed. By 538 B.C.E. the Judeans were free to return to their own land if they chose.

Internally, the displaced Judeans poured over their sacred traditions and texts—their canon. Priests and those known by the scholarly convention as Deuteronomistic historians searched the past in an effort to explain the catastrophe of the Exile and to chart the course for whatever future that might lie ahead. Similarly, Israel's story in the Psalms began to take shape during this new wilderness existence. Old texts were heard in new contexts and in this dialectical engagement between text and community, a particular configuration of canon took hold and a new community was born. It is this canonical process—the energized engagement between ancient texts and subsequent communities—that holds promise for modern congregations.[62]

The shift in congregational studies from the language of "identity" to "culture" is significant because it signals a willingness by some people to understand the peculiar configuration of a religious community as something less than fixed and given.[63] For others, to be sure, this can be a challenging notion—especially those for whom the current social arrangement "works." The order of the society is equated with the order of the cosmos so that the existing social world and the universe are coextensive.[64] For these established individuals, the very possibility that there might be other possible social arrangements never occurs. This particular worldview meshes well with the Christendom Paradigm that Loren Mead describes. But as Mead has seen, this worldview is under massive assault for those who have eyes to see.

Nancy Ammerman's discussion of congregational culture offers a constructive alternative to the Christendom Paradigm for modern congregations. She writes, "congregational culture is more than the sum of what people bring with them and more than a mirror image of the theological tradition they represent. It is a unique creation, constructed out of their interaction together over time."[65] If congregational culture is a

---

[62] On "canonical process" see James A. Sanders, *Canon and Community* (Philadelphia: Fortress, 1984).

[63] See Nancy Ammerman, "Culture and Identity in the Congregation," in Nancy Ammerman, et al., *Studying Congregations: A New Handbook* (Nashville: Abingdon, 1998) 78.

[64] See Peter Berger, *The Sacred Canopy*, 24–25.

[65] Ammerman, "Culture and Identity in the Congregation," 82

"creation," then it is subject to recreation, at least within certain limits. In fact, Israel's acknowledgment of "YHWH reigns!" in the Exile, articulated by Israel's story in the Psalms, represents a radical reconstitution of Israel's community and offers a theological mooring for modern congregations who are struggling with their "identities"/cultures in today's world.

The remarks that follow are intended to help congregations think *theologically* about their mission in a rapidly changing ecology. Ironically, religious bodies are not always led by their theological convictions when making important decisions. Loren Mead tells of this sad state of affairs when he writes:

> A decade ago, a colleague had occasion to do a study of decision making at a group of theological seminaries concerned about their future. He discovered that in no case in his sample did anybody in those seminaries make reference to a theological idea or principle in the decisions that were being made.[66]

Congregations, perhaps most notably in their decisions about resources (e.g., finances, facilities, and personnel), are likewise tempted to act on the basis of what seems to be expedient or desirable rather than on carefully considered theological convictions. The following comments are intended to assist congregations in the utterly serious task and vocational responsibility of theological reflection in today's changing context.

First, "YHWH reigns!" When the Davidic covenant no longer made sense to Israel in Exile, the people returned to and searched their theological resources. They discovered that behind the orthodoxy of God's pledge to David and his family, there were other theological claims to be heard. God graciously responds to particular situations in particular ways. In response to the Philistine threat, the gift of monarchy was one such response. But as the world grew smaller and the imperial forces of Assyria, Babylon, Persia, and, later, Greece and Rome had their ways with Israel and Judah, God led Israel's theologians to a vital rediscovery. The LORD reigns over kingless Israel, even over empires with powerful kings.

What does the affirmation of God's reign mean for today's congregations? At the very least, it means "Don't panic." It is a call to acknowledge that even in a world that may appear very different from the one

---

[66] Loren Mead, *The Once and Future Church: Reinventing the Congregation for A New Mission Frontier* (Washington, D.C.: The Alban Institute, 1991) 56.

into which we were born, God is in control. The Tower of Babel story in Genesis 11 has often, perhaps typically, been read as a tale of God's displeasure with misguided human efforts. In this line of interpretation, the confusion of languages and the dispersal of humankind are seen as divine punishment. Perhaps, however, the greater affront to God was the failure of the people "To be fruitful and multiply, and fill the earth . . ." (Gen 1:28; 9:1). So God mixed things up and sent everybody back out into the world where they were supposed to be in the first place. Pentecost is not the undoing of Babel, as has sometimes been suggested, but rather the acknowledgment that people who speak different languages can, with God's help, understand one another.[67] So congregations in the face of apparent confusion: Don't panic.

On a more challenging note, to acknowledge that God reigns in our day calls for congregations and judicatories prayerfully and thoughtfully to reexamine ancient creeds and confessions. No less than monarchy in Israel, these may well have been God's gift to a particular people for a particular time. However inspired or uninspired these may be construed, no small number of the Church's creeds and confessions arose centuries ago in response to particular situations. Should they be any less subject to critical scrutiny than the creed of the people that Jeremiah challenged as deceptive for their context: "The temple of YHWH, the temple of YHWH, the temple of YHWH"? Surely not.

Of course, the affirmation that "YHWH reigns!" is itself something of a confession. Is it also up for question? For some people the answer will be yes. For most honest people who have not closed their eyes to the horrors of senseless murders, brutality, starvation, disease, and war the question of whether or not God is in control will arise. And it should. But, even to raise the question reveals an act of theological reflection. With most people of faith, the question will eventually land on *how* God reigns. Here different congregations will arrive at different answers. Episcopalians and Congregationalists, Baptists and Methodists, Roman Catholics and Presbyterians will not exhibit their understandings of God's control in identical ways, be they church polity or program. But this should not be taken so much as a problem to overcome as an actuality to be celebrated.

---

[67] For an engaging discussion of Genesis 11 along these lines, see Walter Brueggemann, *Genesis*, Interpretation (Louisville: Westminster/John Knox, 1986).

It takes human community in its greatest diversity—male and female—to show forth the image of God (Gen 1:27). Similarly, it takes the Church in its multiple manifestations to show forth to the world the reign of God. Israel's story in the Psalms does not offer a particular way of enacting God's reign among the peoples of the world. This, then, invites congregations to explore inventive and imaginative ways to show forth the reign of God. What Israel's story does say, however, is that God's reign is to be celebrated with praise.

Second, YHWH creates. As Exilic Israel sought to make sense of its crisis, it probed ancient traditions that took its theologians behind the Davidic covenant to the Mosaic covenant, then to the Abrahamic covenant, and eventually to the memory of God as Creator. Israel situated its own chaos within a universal framework. Indeed, it was only because YHWH was Creator that the Holy One was entitled to reign. Here Israel shared in the thought world of the ancient Near East where the deity powerful enough to establish the world was acknowledged as the reigning monarch.

Actually, ancient Near Eastern creation traditions were more concerned with order than with origins. That is, creator deities in the ancient world typically began their work by dealing with some kind of a "mess" (chaos). Ancient traditions were not terribly concerned with the origin of the "mess," but only that it was there and the creator god brought some sort of order out of the chaos. Israel was no different in this regard as any attentive reader of even the high theology of Genesis 1 will see.[68] For Israel, the opposite of creation was not so much "non-being" as "anti-being."[69] YHWH was the one who assigned hostile forces to their restrained places and allowed for life to flourish. For exilic Israel, this theological understanding made at least two profound claims. First, the power of God was greater than primeval chaos so God was more than capable of ordering the social chaos of the Exile. Second, because the chaotic dimensions of the cosmos were not eliminated but only assigned certain places, Israel's theologians were invited—indeed, driven—to search for the place

---

[68] In Genesis 1 God begins the creative work against the backdrop of an already existing *tōhû* ("formlessness," or "confusion"), *bōhû* ("emptiness"), darkness, and the *tĕhôm* ("watery deep"). The text does not speculate upon where or how these phenomena originated.

[69] See the perceptive essay by Douglas A. Knight, "Cosmogony and Order in the Hebrew Tradition," in Robin W. Lovin and Frank E. Reynolds, eds., *Cosmogny and Ethical Order: New Studies in Comparative Ethics* (Chicago: Chicago University Press, 1985) 139.

of their own chaotic existence within the grand sweep of God's creative purposes.

At the risk of being reductionistic, perhaps it is not too much to claim that the Church—in its multiple and specific configurations—has been far more interested in the "new creation" than in the actual creation within which God has placed it. In keeping this view, the current world is flawed and only some future act of God will correct the problem and save the world. Ecology ("context") has been understood as more of a thing to be conquered and dominated than a gift to cherish and celebrate.[70] Gone is the wonder of the Psalmist: "How many are your works, YHWH! All of them you have made with wisdom; the earth is full of your creatures" (Ps 104:24). What might it mean for today's congregations to recapture this wonder of creation theology that is so much a part of our sacred texts?

Among other things, it would call for congregations to see their own unique cultures as part of the larger ecology of the world and God's concern for the whole world. Mead is correct in his observation that the new mission front is at the congregation's front door, but that should not be taken to mean that the stranger at the door is the enemy to be conquered. To be sure, we are called to proclaim faithfully the Gospel of Jesus Christ. But it may just be that the Gospel is far larger than the sum of the parts that proclaim it and that congregations have much to learn from those who come knocking upon their doors! The heavens, day, and night bear witness to God (Ps 19). An Egyptian princess rescues and nurtures Moses (Exod 2). A Canaanite prostitute named Rahab comes to Israel's rescue as they make their way into the land of Canaan (Josh 2). Cyrus, the Persian king, liberates Israel from its wilderness of Exile (Isa 45). There is absolutely no indication that the Egyptian princess, Rahab, and Cyrus (along with the Ninevites that God delivered in the Book of Jonah) even knew the name of YHWH. But they were very much involved in God's saving purposes. Again, Mead is almost certainly correct in his claim that we can no longer assume most of the people we pass on the street are familiar with the Gospel story.[71] But in view of the biblical claim that all people are created in the divine image and are cherished by God, only an ecclesial

[70] The comments by Lynn White, Jr., "The Historical Roots of Our Ecologic Crisis," *Science* (March 10, 1967) 1203–7.

[71] Mead, *The Once and Future Church,* 50–51.

arrogance of the first degree would say that congregations have nothing to learn about God from their ecologies. Proclaim the Gospel, yes; but listen carefully and attentively. Boundaries exist between the congregation and the world and give definition to the congregation.[72] That is as it should be. But the boundaries need not be as impermeable as some might insist. God may just be trying to get through to the Church. The interaction between a congregational culture and its ecology must be two-way.

The complementary affirmations that "YHWH reigns!" and "YHWH creates!" have implications beyond culture and ecology for congregational life. The congregational frames of leadership and process are also up for reconsideration.

The forced political deprivation of monarchy, accompanied by the rediscovered theological understanding that God, as Creator, is the ultimate source of *leadership* opened new possibilities for Israel. After all, the story of Israel's life under monarchy as told by the multiple voices in the Book of Psalms had not always been that great. With loss came opportunity. So, the privileges and responsibilities that once had belonged exclusively to the reigning monarch were "reassigned" to the larger community. The people as a whole became YHWH's anointed ones (Ps 105:15). Importantly, the Psalter does not cast this democratization of power the same way that Numbers 16 does. There, Korah, Dathan, Abiram, and a number of supporters challenge Moses' leadership by saying that "all of the congregation—all of them are holy—and YHWH is in their midst" (Num 16:3). The following day Moses reverses the charge and the challengers are destroyed. But the changed rhetorical context of the Babylonian Exile calls for a different evaluation. In one of those rare moments in the Book of Psalms when God speaks in the first person, the freedom of YHWH and the crisis of the Exile prompts the words "Do not touch my anointed ones" (Ps 105:15). All of the people are God's anointed.

Among others, Loren Mead and William Diehl have emphasized the increased importance of the laity in this time of the "reemerging" Church.[73] With the mission front at the doors of every congregation, every member becomes—de facto—a missionary. Mission activity is no longer

---

[72] On boundaries see Ammerman, "Culture and Identity in the Congregation," 81.

[73] Mead, *The Once and Future Church,* esp. 49–53; Mead, *Five Challenges for the Once and Future Church* (Washington, D.C.: Alban Institute, 1996) 1–15; William E. Diehl, *Ministry in Daily Life: A Practical Guide for Congregations* (Washington, D.C.: Alban, 1996).

simply a matter of sending specially trained clergy beyond the empire to remote regions, but rather a concern for everyone who walks through the front door of a church building, of a house church, or of a converted bookstore that houses an emerging congregation. How does the middle-aged accountant faithfully represent the Gospel to a colleague whose only impression of Christianity comes from extremists like Jerry Fallwell or from media reports about the sexual scandals in so many congregations? How does the single mother who works two jobs to support her three children nurture her teenage son in the faith when the street gangs seem far more real and captivating to him than the mystery of the sacraments? How does the freshman who leaves for a college on the other side of the country hold on to her identity as a believer without condemning those who believe differently than she? Memorized Bible verses or creeds will no longer do, if in fact they ever did. Members of the Church must become practical theologians who witness to the Gospel where they live, work, and play, and then gather again as congregations to reflect upon the successes, failures, and of just "being" a Christian in this era. Assisting members to engage in this practice of action and reflection calls for intentionality on the part of congregations, as well as denominational colleges and seminaries.

Empowering the laity to be leaders will take different forms in different faith communities. Authority to lead is granted differently by different bodies and can be based on such things as a clear sense of call, reputation, education, gender, sexual orientation, etc. But whatever the criteria for leadership may be for any faith community, the democratizing nudge of the affirmations that God reigns and creates at the very least calls for a reevaluation of those criteria. For Roman Catholics this may mean a serious reconsideration of celibacy and gender requirements involving the ordination of priests for theological reasons and not simply because of the diminishing numbers of parish priests.[74] For some Protestant congregations that are too small to afford ordained, seminary-trained pastors, denominations may have to rethink who is entitled to administer the sacraments. This particular discussion has often been framed by

[74] One source reports "that between 1950 and 2000 the Catholic population increased by 107 percent while the total number of priests increased by only 6 percent" (www.futurechurch.org/fpm/bishops.htm). On June 18, 2000 CNN reported that in 1999 "more priests died than were ordained" (www.cnn.com/2000/US/06/catholic.priest/).

opposing expediency with historical and theological standards. But does not the democratizing impulse of Books Four and Five of the Psalter offer a perspective to reconsider long cherished and guarded theological standards? Just what does it mean for the Church to affirm unflinchingly that God has fashioned all people in the divine image and that God—not socially manufactured systems religiously legitimated—reigns? The question is both frightening and potentially liberating!

The democratizing impulse of the cries "YHWH reigns!" and "YHWH creates!" has implications for *process* as well as leadership. To put it another way, congregations are summoned to remember that there are theological issues at stake when considering "how things get done." Israel's story in Books Four and Five of the Psalter may help guide today's congregations as they struggle to think theologically about process.

Premonarchic Judah had witnessed a massive centralization of political and religious leadership in Jerusalem. In particular, the religious reforms of Josiah in the late seventh century B.C.E.—supported by the theological traditions that appear in the Book of Deuteronomy—bear eloquent testimony to this centralizating tendency (see especially 2 Kgs 23). But hardly forty years later (i.e., 597 B.C.E.), the Babylonian invasion put an end to—or at least radically altered—centralized polity and liturgy. In some ways, the decentering brought on by the Exile is roughly analogous to the scattering of the human community in Genesis 11 after the failed attempt to unite all humankind. That primeval community survived and so did Exilic and postexilic Israel. Vibrant Jewish communities emerged in places like Babylon and Alexandria, Egypt. The former helped crystallize the Hebrew Torah and the latter helped translate the Torah into Greek so that a Hellinized Jewish community could hear and read its Scriptures in its own language. If the scattering of Israel during the Exile is analogous to Babel, the translation of Torah into the various languages of Postexilic Judaism is analogous to Pentecost. Not unimportantly, the Feast of Weeks/Pentecost was associated with God's gift of Torah to the Jewish community. Scattering and diversity did not put an end to God's people Israel.

Israel's story in the Psalms invites congregations not to fear what may appear chaotic. Remember: YHWH reigns, and even that which seems chaotic has a place in God's creation. As congregations open their doors to the communities in and with which they exist, new ideas, new questions, unexpected problems, and unorthodox solutions will walk through those doors. As tradition and threat to tradition meet, tensions arise. Loren Mead has observed that "The Holy Spirit has always represented something unruly to the people of the church. People who love God and love the church are always discovering that the Holy Spirit paints outside the lines we draw to order our church life."[75] This "messy painting" often leads to open conflict. But conflict need not be construed as an evil to be avoided. Carl Dudley writes:

> Conflict only arises when people care about and are committed to each other and the congregation. Consequently, even when conflict is too painful for easy discussion, such episodes can provide valuable learning experiences when participants are willing to work at deciphering the messages that appear in the chaos.[76]

Discerning creative ways to deal with conflict, to make room for multiple voices is vital for today's congregations. To do so is to model what has been given to the Church in its Scripture: multiple voices in the canon. As Nancy Ammerman has documented, the congregational alternative to dealing with conflict is to avoid it, to avoid change, and eventually to die.[77] Exilic Israel chose to engage diversity and conflict and survived.[78]

The story of Israel's reemergence in Books Four and Five of the Psalter also offers instruction for Church judicatories, especially at the denominational level. To put it anachronistically, with the demise of Jerusalem in 587 B.C.E., Israel's "denominational center" was razed to the ground. The elaborate and labor intensive sacrificial worship of the Temple came to a grinding halt. Some priests were carried into exile (e.g., Ezekiel). Doubtless other priestly personnel were left in Jerusalem's ruins, deprived

---

[75] Mead, *Five Challenges for the Once and Future Church*, 34.

[76] Carl S. Dudley, "Process: Dynamics of Congregational Life," in Nancy T. Ammeran, et al., *Studying Congregations*, 119.

[77] Nancy Ammerman, *Congregation and Community* (New Brusnwick, N.J.: Rutgers University Press, 1997) 345.

[78] To be sure, not all exilic and postexilic communities embraced diversity and conflict creatively. Some resisted. Psalm 137 may well represent a bitter retreat to the old party line, as well as do the narrow reforms mandated by Ezra (Ezra 10). But there were other voices to be heard. While it is not likely that the Books of Jonah and Esther *originated* specifically as a counter voice to Ezra, they could—and most surely would by some—have functioned as a daring alternative to an entrenched and narrow nationalism.

of the livelihood they had known before Babylon. The flow of religious leadership ceased to be from Jerusalem to the outlying regions and instead became more centered in various local communities. The process of decision making became more indigenous. As I will note a bit later, Jerusalem remained keenly fixed in Israel's memory. But, the Exile was a graphic reminder that YHWH was not limited to a specific place. As Creator, all of the earth belonged to God (Pss 24, 104).

The changed ecology in which today's congregations find themselves calls for a rethinking of the roles of denominational centers. Mead underscores this when he writes "the national and regional structures designed to send resources far away must change to face the thousands of local situations where the mission frontier touches each congregation."[79] While his is largely a sociological observation, the story of Israel's reemergence in the Psalter offers a theological rationale from which to consider Mead's claim. If all of the earth belongs to God, might we not ask how denominational leadership can bear witness to the universal reign of God by considering creative ways to decentralize and better respond to the current context? Rather than congregations sending significant amounts of money to support the mission as defined by the denomination, what are the ways that denominational structures can financially support the mission that knocks on the congregations' doors? For example, are there ways for congregations and denominations to covenant to allow—indeed, encourage—a percentage of the money normally spent to support the denomination to be used for mission in the local setting? If the local mission effort is congruent with the denominational mission, are not the goals of both served? To be sure, such an arrangement would mean a willingness on the part of the denomination to share authority and decision making processes. But Israel's vitality in its reemergence lay in the Diaspora Jews and not Jerusalem. The urge to construct towers that span the heavens and temples on sacred mountains is strong, indeed, but God seems always to be about the business of sending people away from sacred centers and into the world that the Creator has pronounced to be "Good" (Gen 1). To many, especially those who are ensconced in positions of power, this concept is frightening. But *conversion*, the embracing of and the being embraced by the Gospel, is often frightening.

[79] Mead, *The Once and Future Church*, 59.

With all of this said, Israel's story in the Psalms remembers Jerusalem as a special place in God's world. Psalm 134:3, for example, holds together the cosmos and the city of Jerusalem in its benediction: "May YHWH bless you from Zion, the One who makes heaven and earth." While the rhetorical situation of the Exile called for the decentralization of Israel's social and religious institutions, it did not eradicate the people's fascination with Jerusalem. The disclosure that God was not limited by territorial and political boundaries was an important "rediscovery" for Exilic Israel. Torah proved to be more portable than Temple and Torah fidelity served to guide the Exiles wherever they settled. Indeed, Israel's story as narrated by the Book of Psalms makes this claim as its plot moves from urging obedience to Torah (Ps 1), through the tortured cry of the laments, finally to conclude on a note of resounding praise (Pss 145–150). But Jerusalem still held a special place in Israel's theological imagination and it constituted a source of abiding hope. With liberation from Exile came the freedom to move and, although Diaspora Judaism would continue to grow, the people would periodically make pilgrimage to this special city (Pss 120–134).

To speak of decentralizing denominational hierarchies may sound unnerving to some, but it is neither a call to eliminate places where thoughtful, visionary, and strategic planning occur nor a plea to remove the people involved in such planning. It is, however, a call to enable a two-way pilgrimage and to facilitate the life-sustaining movement of people, ideas, and resources between the headquarters and the congregations. Fundamental to this movement is *trust*. Denominational centers must trust what congregations tell them about congregational ecologies and about the resources needed (e.g., educational materials, financial assistance, and/or guidance, et al.) to proclaim through word and deed the Gospel in their communities. Higher judicatories must also trust congregations to be effective mission agents that don't need the micromanagement of a church executive. At the same time, congregations need to be able to trust that higher church courts have in mind the well-being of every congregation no matter how large or how small, how rural or how urban. This relationship between national headquarters and local congregations is one in which the voice of each partner must be heard and taken seriously. It has to be a relationship of mutuality and support. To be sure, the pilgrimage between center and congregation will be structured differently among the different denomination and faiths. But pilgrimage—at once an acknowledgment of thriving communities away from Jerusalem and at the same time an insistence upon the importance of that same city—became a significant part of Israel's reemergence following the Exile. Likewise, pilgrimage—the dynamic and wholesome interplay between national structures and local congregations—will be vital for the reemerging Church.

Summary

The story of Israel's reemergence after the devastation of the Babylonian destruction was centrally linked to the recovery and reactivation of the ancient traditions that YHWH creates and reigns. The appeal to these ancient tenets of canonical faith within the exilic context provoked a radical reevaluation of all subsequent and derivative creeds. From this ancient and fundamental starting point, Israel was enabled to see its crisis within the universal purposes of God. Simply put, faith in the Creator and reigning God meant that the loss of one particular form of social existence (i.e., monarchy) did not simultaneously mean the end for Israel. To be sure, the ancient traditions of YHWH as king and Creator had to be fleshed out so as to help order life for exilic and postexilic Israel. Major parts of this theological and social reconstruction included the acknowledgment of the loss of monarchy and immediate hope of political autonomy, the reality of the Diaspora with its threats and possibilities, the creative presence of God—especially through Torah—wherever the people might be, and the democratization of the Davidic claims. But in response, Israel could offer praise—a praise that subverted oppression and honored God at one and the same time.

Congregations in today's rapidly changing context/ecology are called to think anew and theologically about their presence in the world. The acknowledgment of God's reign and creative power—a daring act that may well carry congregations, denominations, and faiths behind familiar, dogmatic formulations—has the potential to assist congregations as they ponder issues of culture, ecology, leadership, and process. Different faith communities will arrive at different ways to embody the reign and creative power of God. But perhaps that is as it should be in view of a Creator who made each person unique, yet each person human.

Conclusion

n the preceding pages I have claimed that the Book of Psalms narrates a story of Israel. I have argued for a mode of reading the Psalter that does not discount the value of historical critical inquires, but instead opts for a synchronic approach to reading the Psalms. Accordingly, the multiple voices within the Book of Psalms tell a story that is largely concerned with the emergence, establishment, and collapse of monarchic Israel and the reemergence of Israel following the loss of kingship. It is a story of survival, the loss of and quest for identity, and, for believing communities, a canonical story. Remarkably, Israel's story closely parallels the Church's story in its emergence in a hostile world, its fusion with the Roman Empire, its eventual envelopment by a radically changed context, and its consequent push to rediscover its core identity. This too is a story of survival, the loss of and quest for identity. As the Church's multiple congregations discover their own particular stories within the larger, canonical story of Israel in the Psalms, creative possibilities are unleashed to assist congregations as they ponder their own lives and mission in today's world.

The intersection of Israel's story and congregational stories does not necessarily yield detailed programs that religious bodies can simply appropriate and apply. However, the engagement of Israel's and congregational narratives evokes theological insights that can assist believing communities in their quest for identity and mission in today's context. Intentional theological reflection must precede, accompany, and follow any

143

action or program that is undertaken by the Church. To recall a voice from the Psalter: "Unless the LORD builds the house, those who build it labor in vain" (Ps 127:1—NRSV).

The period of Israel's emergence was a moment of possibilities and choices. Standing at the boundary between wilderness and land, between guidance by Torah/YHWH and human kingship, Israel debated the choices. The possibilities of Torah-YHWH and/or kingship that open Israel's story in the Psalter (Ps 1 and 2) were the subject of an ancient and unsettled debate. Competing voices always existed even as Israel moved ponderously toward monarchy. At the heart of the debate was Israel's allegiance to Torah, and the fundamental rationale of any form of government: "to save my people." Today's congregations are summoned never to lose sight of alternatives, whether they are young and struggling, settled and thriving, declining, or redeveloping. Israel's story in the Psalms reminds congregations that God holds out possibilities for different forms of "being" in different contexts as long as they remember that their existence must be grounded in a dynamic relationship with God's instruction and a dialogical openness to their environments. Furthermore, any action a congregation takes must keep in view the theological mandate, "to save my people."

The period of establishment for Israel's monarchy was not as "established" as might first be thought. Despite the strong—indeed, dominant—voices that proposed and supported monarchy, there were multiple voices that protested human kingship was not the ultimate answer to life's woes. Oppression by enemies, sickness, death, and even the sense of alienation from God were rampant during the period of Israel's establishment. The socially constructed world of monarchy was not a cure-all. But God was not distant and removed; indeed, God chose to act through listening rather than utterance. To be heard is to be granted the permission and power to be whole. Accordingly, today's congregations are urged to cultivate the gifts of restrained speech and passionate listening. Pronouncement must give way to audition if any assertion is to have the capacity for help and healing. God chose not to silence divergent voices, homogenize, or demonize them with such labels as "heresy." Listening congregations—whether emerging, established, declining, or reemerging—are essential for the well-being of Christ's Church.

The episode of Israel's collapse was framed by pained voices that could not be silenced by the optimistic voices that proclaimed the centrality of Zion. In this unsettled moment of Israel's existence, the voice of pain would prevail. Arguments to the contrary proved only to be a temporary detour that always led back to the tortured trail of lament. Whatever future awaited Israel would be found by travelling its own Via Dolorosa. Passionate listening and restrained speech does not mean that the Church must surrender voice. It does, however, mean that the Church must consider carefully who gets to speak. As established congregations witness the collapse of familiar, comfortable structures and struggle for their bearings in a changing world, previously marginalized and hurting voices must be empowered to speak. Truly prophetic voices wait to be heard from the ranks of the laity, from women, and from the victims in the world. The congregation that would bar the doors and hide within only blesses the misery of the world and in the end will perish just as Jerusalem perished under siege. The Church's future lies in unbolting the doors and raising stained-glass windows and empowering the voice of "the Other."

The reemergence of Israel during and following the calamity of the Exile was keenly tied to is reclamation of the twin claims that "YHWH reigns" and "YHWH creates." The acknowledgment of YHWH's universal scope and sovereignty provided the theological underpinnings for a new vision of life after monarchy and in Diaspora. The reign and creative power of YHWH, especially mediated through Torah and occasional pilgrimage to Jerusalem, guided Israel as the people struggled with issues of identity, context, leadership, and process. The result was a new and vital Israel. As congregations find themselves in increasingly unfamiliar surroundings—an exile of sorts—the twin claims of God's creative power and God's reign, mediated through a dynamic canon / Torah, offer valuable theological landmarks for negotiating uncharted waters. To be sure, no denomination or congregation that chooses to follow these landmarks will remain unchallenged or will be guided by them in exactly the same way. But for each religious community that takes these claims seriously, old ways of being and doing will be called into question while new ways of being faithful and proclaiming the Gospel will come into focus. Old systems of hierarchies and power will be amended by new and egalitarian visions of leadership and power that emerge in keeping with a God who has made all humans in the divine image and to whom all humans are ultimately answerable. For those congregations with the vision and the faith to follow the path blazed by Israel's story in the Psalms, a new and vital existence awaits.

A Final Word

It was a story months in the making. Despite being nearly two years apart, Gary and I were the closest in age as kids in the rural congregation where we were members in the 1950s and so we became good friends. About the only time that we saw one another was at church on Sunday mornings. The one big exception was the week of Vacation Bible School when we got to "hang out" five mornings in a row. One year Gary's VBS group got to work with clay—which was no small thing since most of the other groups got only crayons. At one of the long-awaited refreshment breaks that week, Gary challenged me to see who could hit the paneled ceiling inside the church building with a lump of clay. He was older than I and always won the rock throwing contests that took place on the gravel driveway every Sunday. But I didn't think that even Gary could hit the high ceiling in that old weather-boarded church building. When all of the adults and other kids were outside at the refreshment period, we sneaked back inside with our lumps of clay. I went first and, predictably, didn't get close. Then Gary wound up, hurled the clay that hit the ceiling with a big splat—and stuck.

We didn't tell anyone about the contest and hoped that no one noticed that pink clay up on the ceiling, and I'm not sure that anyone ever did. But for the next several months, all that Gary and I could do during worship was to stare at the clay and wonder who it would hit if it fell. We always figured that Mrs. Crosslyn was the most likely target because she sat closest to the "bulls-eye" and wore a huge black hat. Despite our weekly one-hour vigil, the clay stuck fast until one Sunday after worship when I was about to get into the car with my family to go home, Gary came racing out of the church with the clay in his hand. "It fell!" he shouted as he showed me. Mom and Dad didn't know exactly what he was talking about—and we didn't bother to explain!—but Gary and I were silently swept away by the mystery of the moment. Months after the clay had been "launched" it fell on the one morning a week when someone was there, not hitting anyone, and in the presence of the same person who had thrown it. We figured it meant something, but we never could sort out exactly what.

Forty-some years later I still haven't figured out what that episode in life meant because, taken by itself, it was just one of those curious moments that happens to all of us and really doesn't hold much meaning in and of itself. But in the larger narrative of that congregation's life, who knows? Not too long after that lump of clay released its grip on the ceiling, resistant voices in that congregation decided to go along with plans to replace the deteriorating building with a new structure. Subsequent renovations to that building have occurred, sometimes over protest. Members have come and gone—some have been baptized and others buried there. Along with weddings and other joyous celebrations, there have been more than a few battles waged over pastors, money, property, etc. But as I write these lines, I look forward to "a pilgrimage" to that congregation in a few weeks where we will all celebrate my parents' fiftieth wedding anniversary.

The Church exists at a time when "the clay has fallen," when old and familiar structures that we have stared at for so long have collapsed. Amazingly, Israel's story in the Psalms comes to us as one about the emergence, establishment, and collapse of the familiar. But Israel's story also arrives as a tale of reemergence—and as canon. For congregations that have a sense of the dynamic nature of canon, of how the Church can interact creatively and not defensively with its context, and how the Church can welcome all voices into the deeply textured life of faith, there will be ongoing challenges and astonishing celebrations in the decades to come.

Subject Index

Author Index

Index of Psalms Treated